DEMO GURU

THE CREDIBLE VOICE OF THE TECHNICAL SALE

DEMO GURU

THE CREDIBLE VOICE OF THE TECHNICAL SALE

*A Guide to Master the Sales Engineering
Profession to Perfection*

ALESSIO LOLLI

DEMO GURU: THE CREDIBLE VOICE OF THE TECHNICAL SALE A GUIDE TO MASTER THE SALES ENGINEERING PROFESSION TO PERFECTION

iUniverse books may be ordered through booksellers or by contacting:

iUniverse
1663 Liberty Drive
Bloomington, IN 47403
www.iuniverse.com
844-349-9409

ISBN: 978-1-6632-1465-2 (sc)
ISBN: 978-1-6632-1466-9 (e)

Print information available on the last page.

iUniverse rev. date: 12/30/2020

I love when people address me as the "Demo Guy."
And I do not think presales is an art.

Table of Contents

Foreword

By John Care

Co-author of *Mastering Technical Sales: The Sales Engineer's Handbook.*

I, like many Sales Engineers, have always had a love-hate relationship with the product demonstration. On one hand, it is an absolute requirement that at some point in the sales cycle you have to "show your stuff". It is a proof point. Customers demand it.

On the other hand, fully 75% of demonstrations occur too early in the sales cycle, often because the sales team has run out of other options to progress the opportunity. So, it is fundamentally a fact of SE life – you have to live with the dash to demo.

Knowing that fact, and that regardless of how much upfront technical and business discovery you conduct – that demo is still hanging over your head as a step which has to be completed. So why not excel at that step?

This is not just yet another book about demos. It doesn't take 200+ pages to beat a single methodology into your brain.

It is a collection of situational stories, tips, recommendations, and real-life mistakes – all designed to help you change your demo setup and your demo delivery. It is about new behaviors and new habits and a fresh new look at the demo.

What is a rescue demo? What should you consider for a release readiness demo? How do scripted demos differ from the more free form style demos? Just reading and then discussing "Great Demo, But We Lost the Deal" could keep an SE team busy for an entire evening.

Alessio promotes a minimalistic approach to the demo. Show what you need to show with the minimum number of clicks, screens, and words.

Your job is to sell, and to light up the customer's curiosity and their sense of hope – it is not to educate.

I'll leave you with the very first piece of advice I received from a Sales Manager after my very first demo – over three decades ago.

"Sales Engineers do not get paid by the word."

You also don't get paid by the demo; you get paid for the win!

Enjoy the read.

John Care

Managing Director
Mastering Technical Sales
www.masteringtechnicalsales.com

About John

John is currently the Managing Director of Mastering Technical Sales, a company dedicated to serving the Professional Skills needs of Sales Engineers around the world.

John spent numerous years building world-class Sales Engineering organizations at companies such as Oracle, Sybase, Vantive, Clarify, HP, Business Objects and most recently Vice President and Area Manager of Pre-Sales at CA. He has a BSc with Honors in Chemical Engineering from Imperial College, London and is a former contributing member of the MBA Advisory Council for the Fox Business School of Temple University, Philadelphia. He has been published in such diverse media as CIO, InfoWorld, Touchline and The Wall Street Journal.

Preface

Genesis and Style of the Demo Guru

I am not a professional writer, and I would have never thought that one day I would be publishing a book. Here I am, though, on my outdoor deck in NYC, the city I love and have called home for over 10 years, jotting down my very last notes during a humid summer night in the midst of a global pandemic.

I decided to write this manual a year or so ago when I realized how much Sales Engineering has expanded to a highly regarded profession over the last decade, with a healthy network of experienced professionals coming together. The fact that in the last year I have changed roles within my organization might have also accelerated this decision—a way for me to live again some of the best experiences I have ever had in my career.

As a matter of fact, this book comes from experience. As a proud Demo Guru for almost 15 years, I want to share what I have learned with my readers, my successes and my failures, and provide guidance to all those colleagues that just like me share the same passion for evangelizing technology. The "True Story" paragraphs of this book speak just about that: real-life experiences from the fields that help solidify specific concepts, coupled with informative "Recommendation" sections that nourish from those experiences to provide suggestions and guidance. A few "Extra Tips" aim to arm presenters with tricks and insights to maximize their presentation skills and some quick "Top 3 Takeaways" sections help readers summarize and retain the key aspects for each of the topics discussed.

The main audience for this manual is the Sales Engineer, as part of the Presales team. I would also invite, however, Sales Account Executives to take a read. Since Presales is inherently connected to Sales, many of the topics presented in this book naturally involve Account Executives, and

I am confident they also would enjoy hearing the voice of their sidekick. The goal is to create a stronger alliance and a deeper collaboration between two distinct personas that, for the nature of the business itself, tend to experience friction with each other.

The content is meant to be practical yet educational. I am sure many of the situations illustrated in this book will resonate with both experienced Sales Engineers and novice Demo Gurus, inspiring continuous improvement.

The style is meant to be placid yet engaging. The choice of words is mostly industry-agnostic, with specific terminology appealing primarily to the world of B2B Enterprise Software, making it easy to read for anyone demonstrating products and solutions across any business.

I hope you will enjoy reading this book as much as I enjoyed writing it and, most importantly, as much as I enjoyed living its experiences.

#PROUDDEMOGURU

Acknowledgments

In writing this book, I have drawn so much from my professional experience that it would be an act of unfairness not to thank the individuals I have come to personally meet in the last 15 years. All of you have contributed stories and experiences that I relish today, and to all of you I humbly say, Thank You.

I will be forever grateful to my very first boss who believed in me right out of college when I barely knew what a MS Excel spreadsheet looked like. With persistence, patience, and passion, she showed me the way and shaped me into who I am today. Good or bad, for what it is worth, thank you Elena for teaching me "what good looks like."

To my first employer, Tagetik, and its management team who has always acted more as mentors than a reporting line. My deepest gratitude goes out to all of you for making me part of an exciting, invigorating, and at times, stressful-but-extraordinarily-rewarding journey.

As predictable as it might sound, how could one not say thanks to family? The family that many years ago saw me relocate to the other side of the Atlantic Ocean, pushing me to follow my instincts without ever doubting me and inspiring me to responsibly embrace life. GRAZIE.

To my nephews, Francesco and Filippo, who are not able
to read English yet, but that I am sure one day will.

January 2021

PART 1: FUNDAMENTALS OF SALES ENGINEERING

Chapter 1.1 – Introducing the Demo Guru

When talking about my job with some friends a long time ago, a curious listener sitting at a table nearby asked if I was a therapist. I answered that I was not. "I am a software sales engineer." When they asked me what that meant, I explained, "I meet with prospective customers, sit down with them, and listen to their current pains and challenges. I then take some time to process what they tell me and then go back to show how my products and skills can solve their current pains and help them in the future." Just as the words were coming out of my mouth, I realized I was fundamentally describing a therapist.

A therapist is a medical professional who uses a process called "therapy" to remediate a problem, listening to their client's struggles, making a diagnosis, and finally suggesting a course of action.

Demo Gurus are business therapists—we use a process, called the Sales Cycle, to listen to our prospective customers' hurdles and issues. Then, we diagnose them and, only when the time is right, propose a solution called Product Demo.

The more I thought about it, the more similarities I found between the role of a solution engineer, a far more professional-sounding name for a Demo Guru, and the role of a therapist. We both deal with troubled customers searching for a better future, we both rely on our social and communication skills, and we both are gifted with a natural, high degree of empathy and positivity. Furthermore, therapy is not simply an art but an actual science that needs to be studied, internalized and exercised. Sales engineering is not an art, either; it requires study, dedication, and countless hours of practice.

Now, of course, we are dealing with a different level of seriousness and gravity. Medical therapists are commendable human beings who make intelligent use of their skills and qualities to help and frequently save human lives—there is nothing more rewarding than that. Demo Gurus are business therapists who do not save lives but can make them much better for the customers they serve.

The following few pages will describe how Demo Gurus, also referred to as Presales Consultants or Sales Engineers, should consult with their prospective customers.

We will start by first explaining the skills required to be an outstanding Demo Guru.

We will then analyze how Demo Gurus participate in the overall sales cycle, the role they play, and the value they bring throughout its many steps.

Finally, we will wrap it up with some basic suggestions on how to embrace and master this profession to excellence.

Let's get started!

What Sales Engineers Do and Do Not Do

Sales Engineers consult. Salespeople sell. If you were to remember anything out of this book, remember these five words: SALES ENGINEERS CONSULT. SALESPEOPLE SELL.

The main role of sales engineers during the sales cycle is to represent the "credible" side of the sale. We are not saying salespeople are not credible enough or, even worse, are cheaters. The stereotype that is commonly attached to salespeople's profiles does, however, not play to their advantage. Try typing "sales reps are" in your Google search bar and you will find the suggested search results are less than flattering:

Figure 1.1.1. Web Browser Search

Just like with any stereotype, it does not mean that every salesperson is lazy, annoying, or simply aiming to book a sale. Unfortunately, however, that is the perception we all have when getting in touch with salespeople, and it is even more true in the area of Software Sales.

It is on us, the Demo Gurus, to counterbalance that perception. Sales engineers' primary responsibility is to act as trusted advisors for their prospective customers, advising them on how the solution they are representing could help with the customers' challenges and elevating themselves to the role of Subject Matter Experts (SMEs). Sales engineers will undoubtedly possess extensive knowledge of the products and solutions they will demonstrate, but most importantly, they will consult on best practices and market and industry trends so their customers can learn from them and ultimately trust them.

How do we gain the trust of our future customers? The actual demo, which quite understandably feeds the typical stereotype of presales being just demo machines, is only one of the tools sales engineers have at their disposal to establish themselves as Trusted Advisors.

Relying on the demo meeting to establish your credibility and trustworthiness might be a bit "too little too late."

Building your reputation as a Trusted Advisor starts the very moment you have been assigned an opportunity. From that moment on, you will initiate contact with your prospective customer multiple times before the actual demonstration—through discovery calls, clarification calls, presentation dry runs, etc.—with the sole intent of understanding your customer's needs so that you can bring the most value to them.

Sales engineers that succeed in establishing themselves as trusted subject matter experts are those that your prospective customers would like to work with, whether they end up buying your solution or not.

With customers perceiving them as knowledgeable and credible resources they would enjoy doing business with, Demo Gurus become the quarterback of any company's go-to-market strategy. We will be talking more in detail in the next few chapters about how presales can help the entire organization beyond simply delivering demos.

For now, let's just point out that Demo Gurus do not simply do demos. Demo Gurus generally reside inside the Sales organization and interact with all key business areas. The image below shows how a sales engineer's mind should operate for optimal performance (time allocation might vary depending on specific product maturity):

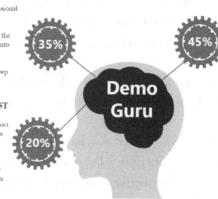

INDUSTRY EXPERT

Active Networker – with a professional and credible personal brand

Competition Specialist – studies the competition to get better insights into strengths and weaknesses

Subject Matter Expert – gains deep business and technical experience

PRODUCT EVANGELIST

Content Creator – supports product marketing with messaging and sales materials

Product Innovator – collaborates with product management for new features and product enhancements

TECHNICAL SALES PRO

Relationship Builder – charismatic and likeable, both inside and outside the organization

Exceptional Presenter – engaging style for customer presentations and other speaking events

Expert Storyteller – communicates in a simple way through past experiences

Hands On Techie – spends significant amount of time implementing and troubleshooting software solutions to meet customer's requirements

Commercially Savvy – understands the dynamics of the sales cycles

AE Sidekick: collaborates and supports the assigned Sales Person to book the sale

Figure 1.1.2. Presales Areas of Intervention

Sales engineers' best friends and worst enemies are their assigned salesperson, hence why we have decided to dedicate a full chapter to this complex and intense relationship! Usually, one presales professional tends to help two to three outside sales representatives, causing a roller coaster of emotions. From pure love when a contract is signed to genuine frustration when account executives miss tracking their customers' conversations on the CRM or the presales resource does not do enough demo-customization, sales engineers support their salesperson along the entire sales cycle. They help select the most appropriate follow up material and identify the best references, going the extra mile with custom documentation and offering deep-dive meetings. Sales engineers are as emotionally invested in the sales cycle as their salespeople.

Beyond sales, Demo Gurus leverage their constant presence in the field to help their marketing, product management, and competitive intelligence teams become evangelists for their company and its solutions.

Must Haves for Sales Engineers

I do not believe that sales engineers are a special breed; I believe most of the qualities that make a sales engineer a successful player are very similar to what would make any eager professional succeed in business life. The only difference with sales engineers is that for them to be successful, they have to focus on convincing others to appreciate and trust them.

Being a successful sales engineer involves winning over your prospective customers; to do so, here are five must-have qualities that each Demo Guru should naturally be gifted with or develop over time, if possible:

- Passion: You must be a charismatic and energetic individual who enjoys what you are talking about and can proudly demonstrate how your solution is the best in the market. You are passionate about your company, its people, and its offerings; your audience can feel you are genuinely invested in your job and sees you as an evangelist of the organization and the product they are evaluating. It is not just enough to be passionate about your product if your prospective customers cannot feel it themselves through your words, gestures, and behaviors.

- Curiosity: You must want to learn more and have a desire to go the extra mile—you must be truly interested in how your prospective customers operate and what is impeding their success today. Just like your prospective customers highly appreciate the passion you have for what you do, which is visible during your presentation, they will also value your curiosity during your demonstration. The research you have done, the information you have gathered, and all the scouting or investigation you have completed on their current situation, you did it for them—to better serve them and to better understand their reality. Your prospect will, without any doubt, acknowledge your due diligence.

- <u>Creativity:</u> You must have strong analytical thinking capabilities and be able to quickly think outside of the box, tapping into lateral, unknown areas that could bring additional value to your prospective customer. I always use a simple metaphor with my junior presales resources: "Your prospect will hand you a brick, and you will have to build a castle out of it." While the expression "thinking outside of the box" might seem over-used and mostly a buzzword since no scientific formula for how to accomplish this is generally provided, critical thinking is reality. Do not stop at what you are told; go behind the scenes and dig into the reason why you have been told something. Explore different, alternative approaches to reach the same result with a higher value.

- <u>Attention to Details:</u> You must pay close attention to details. This is one of the main qualities I try to assess during an interview. Details make the difference, and you have to be different. It is a true story that Steve Jobs, CEO of the most valuable American company, Apple, called Vic Gundrotta, the man behind Google +, on a Sunday morning in 2008 to have him fix the gradient of the second O in the Google logo that appeared on the iPhone back then. Developing a mindset that is naturally geared to pay attention to details will boost your critical thinking skills, allowing you to venture into areas and discussions that your competition has not even remotely considered but that your prospects will appreciate immensely.

- <u>Communication Skills:</u> Your job is all about listening to your prospective customer's needs and communicating the value your solutions will bring to them. Both verbal and non-verbal communication skills are vital for your success as an outstanding sales engineer, hence why again we have decided to dedicate a full chapter to this! Your positive attitude towards problem-solving and the energy you bring to the table will make you a likable person with whom your prospect will enjoy working.

Show empathy, open-mindedness, and interest when entering a dialogue with your audience by being flexible and open to listen to the other person's point of view. Show confidence, determination, and courteous authority when expressing your personal views on any given matter, both with your words and your body language.

True Story – My #1 Competitor

Realistically, out of the five must-haves described above, communication and social skills are the qualities that are the easiest to develop and nourish for a Sales Engineer. I have run into a few of my coworkers that when I initially hired them, I would have never thought they would one day become exceptional presenters. You might be asking yourself why I hired them in the first place. The answer is that I have never been a champion at hiring; probably the best I have done with hiring is delegating the task to somebody else. A few years ago, however, I hired this young person right out of college. We started our journey together and then we had the first demo rehearsal; an internal presentation to just myself to assess where we stood in terms of presentation skills. It was not good, so we kept working on it. Months went by, and I was starting to get very skeptical, but this young professional did not give up. With determination and an incredible amount of hours spent reading about presentation techniques and an equally incredible amount of hours spent practicing, I can proudly say this person is now one of my toughest competitors when it comes to presentation and communication skills.

Chapter 1.2 – Understanding the Sales Cycle

This chapter should be focusing on the Buyer's Journey rather than the Sales Process. Only through a critical understanding of how buyers show intent, research, and shop for a solution will it be possible for any sales professional to maximize their sales efforts.

In the next few pages, we will not be going into the details of how to manage a sales cycle, which is not the direct responsibility of any Demo Guru. We will instead focus on a few areas of the sales process that are vital for sales engineers to become familiar with and answer questions like "How did we get this lead?" and "What happened to that customer we demoed to last week?"

Before we get too deep into it, let me just clarify one topic: always assume your future buyer is mostly an EDUCATED buyer. Today's overwhelming amount of free information allows prospective buyers to do their research before reaching out to you. Not only will they be very clear about what they want, but most will probably be very knowledgeable about what they want and can do, what the market is offering, and what your strengths and weaknesses are when compared to the competition. Prospective buyers today typically go through an extensive amount of research and self-education before reaching out to vendors.

What this means for your organization and yourself in particular is the following:

- Your lead generation department should focus on creating needs for those potential buyers that have not started their self-education yet to model and influence their ad hoc research. In other words, focusing on early "intent" rather than opportunistic "website downloads" to maximize targeting.

- Your marketing and customer success departments have to invest in getting positive branding and becoming reputable from information that is not "company provided." It is far more effective for potential buyers to consult independent user reviews of your solutions, analyst ratings, customer testimonials, employee social media postings, and in general, any other information about your solution not directly coming from your company itself.

- Specifically, as a Demo Guru, you need to do at least the same amount of research on your prospective customer's company and needs that they have done for your company and solution. If only to return the favor, you have to invest a considerable amount of time understanding what triggered their needs, what pain points they are trying to fix, their timeline, their expectations, their ultimate success criteria, etc., so you can tailor your sales efforts to meet their exact needs.

Tailoring your sales efforts to the buyers' needs means showing them VALUE. As much as this is a truth universally acknowledged, very little time is spent on selling value rather than product features and functions.

Focusing on functionality will make you lose the deal for two very basic reasons:

1. *No one cares about your product.* If that is true, and believe me, it is, how come every prospect will want to rush to a demo and see your product in action? In reality, what they are doing by asking for a demo is trying to understand how your product will solve their problems and create VALUE for them. Prospects are rushing to the demo because vendors usually talk about themselves, how powerful their product is, how visionary their company is, etc. Therefore, prospects want to see it for themselves—rightfully so. They are asking for a demo right away because they are anxious to uncover what value your solution brings to them, which typically software vendors tend to invest little time in explaining. Move the conversation from US to THEM. Focus on THEM and explain how your company and solution will create VALUE for them and make them successful. Position your product as an enabler for value creation.

2. *Your product is very similar to many others.* I might be hurting your ego now, but you need to come to this realization. As proud and passionate as you are about your product, and unless you are operating in a monopoly environment, chances are that your competitors provide functionalities that are extremely similar to yours. In software sales, there is nothing to be proud of when it comes to Data Integration or Data Visualization—hundreds of companies out there have at least the same set of features and functions. Maybe some even better. Focusing on features and functions will not get you anywhere but to a beauty-contest and pricing-battle field. On the contrary, use your best product functionality as a launching pad to position and deliver value to your prospect. Explain to them how you can help them with their needs and open their eyes to areas they have not considered.

True Story – Learning From My Mistakes

The realization that features and functions are not that effective in piquing the customer's interest came to me after a few years of hands-on experience as a Demo Guru. Not because no one told me before: I simply projected my sense of pride and passion for specific features that ended up not being of interest to my prospects. In Boston, MA, I was performing a demo for a publishing company. After maybe ten minutes of me talking, I was interrupted by one of the attendees. With firm resolution, she openly told me I would not be sitting at that table if they thought we did not have what I was proudly showing them. She also suggested to either show them what it would take to set up that particular functionality or, better yet, explain to them how it would help them. She clearly was not interested in the functionality, per se. My take-away? First, always relate what you are showing to the needs of your prospects. Second, ask before drilling into too many details.

Now that we have understood that value creation is at the basis of any sales cycle, let's try to understand what happens before we receive a request for demo from our account executive and what usually takes place after our demo(s).

Figure 1.2.1. Sales Activities Before and After Demo Day

It all starts with the right MARKET DEFINITION to establish what our target customer is and to what buying personas we are going to offer our solution. Defining a target market can be done in multiple ways, which we will not examine in this book. Suffice it to say the market definition is what drives your positioning, your product development, and therefore your sales. Target markets for global organizations are usually identified by Company Size (typically in terms of Revenue, Number of Employees or Assets for Financial Services organizations)

13

and Industry (Manufacturing, Banking, Professional Services, etc.) Given a specific target of company size and industries, it is key to identify to which buying profiles our solution will appeal and identify specific messaging for that specific persona. For example, a C-level executive usually has different needs than a very specialized Analyst, yet we might have to market to both if the buying process relies on a communal selection. It is fundamental to identify what specific target and demographics our product appeals to (the so-called "sweet spot") to maximize our sales efforts.

Once we know our target market, the next step is all about LEAD GENERATION. This is where an Inside Sales department, or an SDR (Sales Development Representative) organization comes into play. Historically seen as the first stage of any career in sales, SDR teams work closely with the marketing team to generate leads by typically being the first ones making contact with a prospective customer. Leveraging both the many campaigns and initiatives that the marketing colleagues constantly run and the top-of-the-line lead generation software that helps identify contacts within any target organization, SDRs have the tough job of initiating a call and convincing the prospective customer to commit to a future meeting. If done properly, this is not just about scheduling an appointment; there is instead a tremendous amount of research, investigation, and preparation before a call is made to ensure the message is relevant to the target company. During their conversations, SDRs try to understand if the prospective customer has a real buying intention, or if the account needs to simply be nurtured as 'not yet ready to buy.' Based on the very frequent B2B sales best practice of BANT screening, SDRs try to uncover if the prospective customer has enough Budget, Authority, Need, and an appropriate Timeline for a decision in their interactions with the prospective buyers. If all four (or sometimes three out of the four) criteria is met, the prospective customer is commonly marked as an SQL, or Sales Qualified Lead, and passed on to the Account Executive (AE) to advance the sales cycle.

Once in the AE's hands, the SQL generated by the Inside Sales Team usually goes through an OPPORTUNITY QUALIFICATION to make sure the account is workable and therefore converted from an SQL to a QSO, or Qualified Sales Opportunity. Erroneously, it is commonly believed that this is when the sales process starts, now that there is an active opportunity to work on. In reality, as an organization, our sales efforts started months before when the marketing and SDR teams created interest and solidified that interest to the point that a prospective customer was willing to meet with the always-dreaded Account Executives. With an active opportunity to work on, the AE will further advance his/her deal qualification while positioning our solution through a set of value drivers that resonate specifically with the audience. At the right time, the AE will involve the presales engineer to deep dive and discover more about the prospective buyer's needs while still solidifying the relationship with them. The AE will typically substantiate his/her messaging, positioning, and value statement through documentation and collaterals and, just as a proof point, will offer up a product demonstration to the prospective customer.

Now that we have all the information and have socialized the prospective customer to our solutions and the value they will bring to them, it's time for DEMO DAY. Since demonstrations are one of the core topics of this book, we will keep this paragraph short for now as much more will be said about Demo Day in chapter 2.3.

If the demo has met its main objective of conveying what the team has been positioning in the prior interactions, the prospective customer will want to learn more and will want to talk to existing customers with similar needs to learn about your company and solution. This is usually referred to as REFERENCE CHECKING. This step in the sales cycle should not be underestimated, as it is one of the most critical selling techniques your AEs should use to seal any deal. As usual, it is fundamental to prepare both the prospective customer and the current customer to make their conversation as efficient as possible. The first thing your AE should do, even before thinking about which customers to reach out to as a reference, is create a "value statement" for the prospective customer. The value statement is a simple one-pager that states why your solution and your organization can create value for them. In the area of software sales, I recommend adding an AS-IS versus a TO-BE graphical representation to show how we have captured their vision and how realistically we will make it happen. In securing references, the AE should rely on the Customer Success department to prepare the existing customers for the reference call by providing them a synopsis of the prospective buyer and any additional info that might help them "sell on our behalf!" Similarly, it is advisable to present a quick overview of the existing customers' profile the prospective buyer will talk to in order to better understand *how* the references are using our solution. Be prepared to have your references address non-product questions! Even if your prospect insists that they want to evaluate how your customers are using your solution, much of the conversation will be off-product and on topics like the quality of your delivery, organization, support, availability of key resources, etc.

If the entire sales organization has done a good job, the prospective customer will undoubtedly choose our solution and organization to partner with for their upcoming initiative, and we are officially labeled as the VOC, or Vendor of Choice. The moment we are told we are VOC is the best and worst moment of the sales cycle. It is the best moment for the Presales organization as there is probably no more need for additional demonstration and excruciating product proof points. It is the worst moment for the Account Executive because now the real NEGOTIATION phase of the deal cycle starts. This is when the Sales Rep will have to negotiate the deal both from a commercial and legal perspective, usually involving the company's legal department for contract review and redlining. Both aspects of this negotiation are equally important and could be extremely long and detailed. It is not just a matter of applying a discount to get a deal done; very frequently, sales reps in this phase have to negotiate with procurement departments that might not necessarily be accustomed to buying the type of solution you are offering, making the process a painful, educational journey on which the rep needs to embark.

This is also when AEs might be asked to help their sponsor present a valid ROI for the price tag the AE is asking. Moreover, as it always happens, the AE will also have to deal with last-minute budget cuts, revised scope, loss of interest, and unethical competitive moves that could cannibalize the original deal size. On the legal side of the negotiation, the AE will act as a coordinator between your legal department and the prospective customer's legal department (supposing there is one) or an external attorney, which would complicate things even further. During this phase, both legal teams will agree on contractual terms such as copyright, liability, indemnification, etc. to protect both parties in case something goes wrong. Be careful to address the areas that are absolute non-negotiables for your corporation's standards, and make sure to iron those out before reviewing any additional conditions.

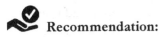 **Recommendation:**

Business to Business selling is inflated with acronyms. SDR, VOC MQL, SQL, QSO, etc. are just metrics that are exclusively relevant to the vendor to assess the productivity, quality, and velocity of its sales process and bring no value at all to the target customer. If anything, all these intermediate steps and actors further stretch the sales process with the risk for the buyer to become annoyed by having to talk and sometimes repeat the same conversations to multiple people. While buyers of Enterprise Software Solutions expect to talk to several individuals within an organization, your sales organization should be very sensitive to this aspect and avoid making your customers feel passed around. Make sure you do not ask questions that have already been asked by anyone else before you in past conversations. Read your SDR notes, log yours for further review, and act as a coordinated team, making it a point to give something back and create value for your prospective customers at every interaction you have with them as a team.

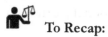 **To Recap:**

The following table shows the level of engagement expected by presales professionals throughout the entire sales cycle and some hints on their main responsibilities for each step of the buying journey.

STAGE IN THE SALE CYCLE	SE INVOLVEMENT	ACTIVITIES, EXPECTATIONS & RESPONSIBILITIES
Market Definition	Low	Your Marketing & Strategy teams will do most of the work here. Sit back.
Lead Generation	Low	Your Inside Sales (IS) team will be hitting the phone to get you a chance to present. Relax.
Opportunity Qualification	Medium	Time to validate your IS lead is a good fit! Your sales counterpart might ask for your opinion on whether or not a lead from the IS team is worth chasing. Some basic due diligence work required.
RFP	High	As a Subject Matter Expert, you will be actively contributing to any product-related info that is required as part of the RFP process.
Discovery Call	High	Clear your throat! From now on, it is all about building credibility and trust with your audience.
Opportunity Plan	Medium	Use this time to work with your sales counterpart of the strategy to win this account: political map, buying process, value proposition, demo flow, etc.

Intro Demo	High	You are on! Your major responsibility is to connect with your audience through value selling and keep them engaged throughout the presentation.
Deep Dive Demo/POC	High	Pressure is on! It is now time to go into proof-mode and show your audience exactly what they want to see.
Reference Checking	Medium	Your Customer Success Department could use some help in identifying the best reference your prospective customer will have a chat with.
VOC Confirmation	Low	Enjoy and have a drink of your choice!
Negotiation & Close	Low	Ask your sales counterpart if there is anything you can help with.
Transition to CS & PS	Medium	It is always a good idea to spend a few hours with your colleagues in Customer Success and Professional Services once a deal is signed to inform them of your findings during the sales process.

Table 1.2.1. Presales Engagement in Sales Cycle

Chapter 1.3 – Selling in the New Normal

The global events that have taken place starting in February 2020 have utterly re-shaped our lives as humans and professionals.

In the last decade, we have been experiencing an increasing demand for virtual selling through screen-sharing platforms, allowing us to leverage remote selling as part of our overall sales strategy. Even before the global pandemic of early 2020, it was not unusual to perform an initial demonstration via the web and visit the prospective customer onsite only when the deal was more qualified.

In the traditional world of enterprise software solutions, it was, however, fairly unusual to finalize a sale without a customer visit by the Account Executive, at least to "put a name to a face." Not that it was ever impossible—I still remember one of the reps I used to work with mentioning a deal that was fully run remotely as a "nice-to-know" item on his Win Report!

Practically overnight, we have been forced to run any sales cycle virtually. What was the exception before became the norm for quite some time. Sales teams around the globe accelerated a practice with which they were already familiar.

But how did the buyers react?

- Buyers seemed confused. Almost all vendors reverted to digital channels to share information, substantially increasing their online presence and content distribution. This resulted in an overflow of similar data points with no real differentiation. Buyers found themselves overwhelmed with information that was less comparable because it was almost identical, shifting their focus to other non-product aspects such as brand awareness, company viability, and vendor's customer satisfaction.

- Buyers reverted to self-education. Because of the massive lack of differentiation that vendors flooded the market with, and probably also having a bit more time available to themselves while working remotely, buyers spent more time researching products and solutions online. It is not surprising how many Business Development departments at the beginning of the global pandemic were reporting a considerable amount of web traffic but could not schedule meetings. Prospective buyers took the time to investigate market solutions and closely compare options.

- Buyers still have needs. This is probably the most important point that has been underestimated by many sales professionals, especially at the beginning of the global pandemic. Yes, many companies put their projects on hold. Yes, many organizations implemented tight cost-control policies. Yes, many enterprises reprioritized investments. But all these approaches did only one thing to your prospective buyers: made their original pains and challenges even more pressing. Your buyer still has needs, and those needs are now even more urgent than before.

How can we, as Sales Engineers and Account Executives, help our buyers?

1. *Position Value.* Now, more than ever, the discussion cannot be based solely or primarily on product features and functions. Your buyers have been bombarded with similar stories and messaging by the competition, and you need to find the angle that reveals the consequences their business could face if they delay fixing the problem they called you for initially. Call for a C-level meeting and prepare for that meeting strategically. Presales, Sales, Subject Matter Experts, and probably even executive representatives from your company should all come together and put on your future customer's hat. The result of this session will be a clear message: Why *now* is the most appropriate time to adopt your product as a key enabler for their organization's well-being and market advantage.

2. *Show Empathy.* This is all about the ability to understand or feel the experiences of another person from their perspective. It's about putting yourself in your buyers' position and viewing the situation through their eyes. The more you can connect with your prospective customers, the better they will trust you and believe in your ability to help them. How can you achieve that? Through Active Listening. A recent LinkedIn survey showed that 47% of buyers look for active listening from their sales counterparts—the highest percentage of all requests submitted. Technology Proficiency only scored an ailing 26%.

3. *Master Relationships.* In the world of highly educated buyers, the old saying in selling "Fake it until you make it" could not be more wrong. Establish yourself as a trusted advisor by being genuine. Connect with your audience beyond pricing and product functionality by showing empathy and building personal connections. Go the extra mile to present a solution to your potential customer's needs by being human. Inviting your

customers to a baseball game is not mastering relationships; being there when they need you the most is.

True Story – The Never-ending Demo

During the late summer months of 2020, when many corporate offices were still on lockdown, I received a call from my Head of Sales mentioning a very large opportunity on the West Coast that was about to advance to the selection phase for a legacy solution replacement. We were invited to demonstrate our solution. Even though we were very late to the process, which is never optimal, I was happy we had a chance to compete until my colleague said the customer was requiring a 9-hour web presentation. After trying repeatedly to dissuade the project leader on the customer side to have her team sit on such a long presentation, all we could do was prepare for the demo and do our best. The great majority of the preparation time was on the scenarios and use cases the prospect sent over that we had to replicate in our solution. As a team, however, we did worry about how to keep the audience engaged and strategized on a few aspects to make the long meeting more digestible. First, we decided to divide the whole demo into 5 main sections of 90 minutes each. Each section addressed a specific set of use cases, introduced by a customer story and followed by a 4-slide deck to recap its most salient points. Additionally, we decided to call for breaks in between sections and assigned our AE to be the moderator, ensuring we dedicated an appropriate amount of time to each section. Our AE was also in charge of reaching out to the audience via the web-chat to make sure we were hitting the mark. On a separate phone chat, my team and I were always up to speed with their private feedback to the AE so we could adjust on the fly. Lastly, we had the great idea of having one of our happiest customers jump in on the meeting and talk live about their experience with us. The prospective customer was surprisingly very engaged and remained in attendance throughout the entire meeting, asking questions and requesting clarifications.

In the era of virtual selling, presales professionals can further establish themselves as thought-leaders and industry veterans by simply educating their prospects on how to conduct effective meetings remotely. It is always a good idea to shorten the distance between the presenter and the audience, even more so in today's physically-distant world.

- Make sure you activate your camera at least during your quick intro. Leverage a white-boarding software tool that allows you to clarify items and topics using basic visuals or diagrams. It is also a good idea to familiarize yourself with the many collaborative features of your screen-sharing platform like breakout room, annotation functionality, polling tools, private chatting, etc.

- Optimize your camera settings and make sure you position it so that it is not too low or too high. Your camera should be at eye level to show your face in full and avoid unflattering angles. When speaking, pretend your audience is the lighted icon on your camera device – this will ensure your prospective customer feels like you are directly addressing them contributing to engagement and retention.

- Use any scheduled breaks to connect with your audience: share personal stories, bring external contributors such as your closest customers to just say a quick hello, or even take a second to show your work-from-home set-up.

The key is to humanize the experience. Do not just talk and click.

 **Extra Tip!**

Build your brand. We live in a digital era, and buyers expect to learn more—not only about your company but about its people as well. As an ambassador for your organization, make an effort to be part of online professional groups, communities, or networks to reinforce the image of Trusted Advisor you want to convey to your audience. Posting or sharing relevant professional content and having your peers endorse your work and skills are just a few highly rewarding ways to solidify your credibility and reputation.

Chapter 1.4 – It Is All About Storytelling

There is no better way to humanize any sales cycle than bringing real life experience in the form of customer stories. Nothing new, yet still an aspect that is largely disregarded in enterprise sales.

Storytelling is a powerful technique to gain credibility, show subject matter expertise, and connect with your audience. It focuses on presenting stories from other customers that are already leveraging your solutions and services, aiming to comfort your audience, prove to them that you have addressed similar concerns and pains already, and show what outcomes and benefits other peers in the industry have achieved.

Have you ever wondered why TED Talks are so captivating and intriguing? Simply put, TED Talks are great examples of storytelling where the presenter aims to make clear points through the use of often personal stories.

If the effectiveness of TED Talks does not convince you enough on how powerful and persuasive storytelling is, maybe science will.

Much of the neuroscience in the past two decades shows us that emotional story-connection activates seven regions of the human brain while data only activates two regions. What this means is that if you are only trying to rationally and logically influence your buyer's decisions, chances are that it will not be enough. To make it even more clear: human beings retain 65 to 70 percent of information shared through stories, while only 5 to10 percent of information is retained through dry presentation of data and statistics.

Let's prove the importance of storytelling with these two simple examples of sales pitches:

Example One:

"Our solution was voted number one in customer satisfaction and has won five awards in the last two months. It is 33% better than solution X. It saves time and money and helps you be more efficient and get your weekends back."

Example Two:

"Mary at ABC Corp. switched to our solution from product X two months ago and said she has already saved 15 hours in reporting hours per week and almost $5,000 in savings. Mary even got a promotion for sponsoring the transition to our solution, and the entire team loves it!"

I am willing to bet that the second example is a better sales pitch. Both examples contain the same information, but the second uses a storytelling approach to make the same points, which makes it easier for the human mind to process and retain.

Just like anything else, storytelling needs preparation and practice.

Storytelling is not a case study in the form of a PowerPoint slide or a marketing brochure. The moment you use those tools to narrate a customer experience, you are "manufacturing" a story, which no longer looks authentic and spontaneous.

For storytelling to be effective, it needs to be delivered naturally and in a genuine fashion. In other words, it needs to be part of the conversation.

Stories also provide a great opportunity to the Account Executive to jump in during the presentation when the Sales Engineer is demonstrating specific features. The additional context and real-life examples will help the audience bridge the gap between what is being demonstrated and the outcome or benefits that they will be getting by adopting that functionality. It also helps break up the demo with a different voice, re-invigorate the attention of those attendees that might have lost interest while also giving the Demo Guru some breathing room.

True Story – Storytelling to the Extreme

I have always been a fan of having our customers sell on our behalf! In a few sales cycles, I have involved some of our best customers to tell their story about their experience with our solution beyond the standard reference-checking process. I have been able to organize site visits where the prospective customer physically meets with our current customers to discuss their use of our solution, sometimes even receiving a real-life demo from the customer on how they use our solution.

Recently, given the travel ban that the 2020 pandemic has imposed on all of us, we were able to have a customer of ours attend a marathon demonstration to a prospective client. This was not easy to accomplish given their Procurement Department not being in love with our suggestion to have one of our customers participate in the meeting to show how they used our solution and talk effectively to their experience with our product. However, the Business Team from the prospective client loved the idea. The two teams spent almost an hour on the phone, in the middle of a product demonstration, talking about the common challenges they both experienced and how our solution was able to overcome them, while my team listened silently.

Huge thanks to my CS Team for making our customers fanatic about our company and product!

The story you will want to report should not be a 20-minute narration of a past project; instead, it needs to be delivered quickly and be right on point.

Usually, the average audience would perceive anything more than 60 or 90 seconds as a disruption to the product demo, so the recommendation is to provide an anecdote that is short, factual, and inspiring with the following content:

STRUCTURE OF A 60-90 SECOND CUSTOMER STORY	
Context	Indicate Customer and Industry you are referring to. If possible, also refer to a specific individual by name
AS-IS Pre-Condition	Explain the situation that the customer was trying to overcome and the challenges to fix
TO-BE Vision	Mention the goal the customer had in mind and what they wanted to achieve
Solution	Simply state your solution delivered on your customer's vision – nothing more required here
Results	Solidify your statement with quantifiable metrics.

As a last reminder, avoid being obvious when telling stories.

Stay away from generic statements like *"ABC Corp. became very effective and efficient at reporting with our solution, drastically reducing their TCO."*

This type of narration can be found on any marketing brochure you will send as a follow up after your meeting. Now that you have the undivided attention from your audience, make sure you use it wisely by being concise, factual, and value-oriented.

 **Extra Tip!**

Have a running list of the most frequent features you tend to show during a demonstration. For each feature, try to find a customer story that factually proves how that functionality works and the benefits that customer experienced when adopting that feature. Share that list with your sales counterpart and invite him or her to jump in during the presentation anytime you happen to demonstrate that feature.

PART 2: EXCELLENCE IN SALES ENGINEERING

Chapter 2.1 – Mastering the Presales Process

It's our turn in the sales cycle. We just got a call from the Sales Rep, and we need to prepare for our moment to shine. Our CEO knows about this, and the pressure is on: we need to excel every step of the way. The most intriguing aspect of excellence is that it is impossible to achieve— no matter how good you are, you can always do better. Aristotle used to say that excellence "is not an act but a habit," a habit being a constant practice mastered to perfection. This chapter examines the typical areas of responsibility for any Sales Engineer and how to master them to perfection.

First Things First

Before diving deep into the many aspects of presales that should be mastered to perfection, let's spend just a couple of minutes discussing something very basic that is usually a given but is often surprisingly by-passed. I call it "knowing the basics" first.

Know the basics

We have already covered how important it is for your prospects to see you as their trusted advisor who can help them solve their problems.

When you visit a prospect, you will establish yourself as an enthusiastic company evangelist and a credible educator by first being able to show your experience working with, and demonstrating knowledge on, your company, your product, your market (and theirs), and your competitors.

1. *Your Company*: You have to know the company you work for, and that goes beyond its legal name and HQ address. You have to live and breathe its values, its mission, its culture, and its roots to spread your company's DNA with any word you use or any action you take. Take a look at your company logo and make sure you know the story behind it.

2. *Your Product*: This is a no brainer. You are in that meeting to show your product; of course you know all about it. Think about what you *really* know: Is it really your product that you are an expert at, or is it more a demo script that you have mastered? Knowing a demo script won't do and is not enough. Just like it is simply not an excuse to say you did not get enough training to go beyond the demo script. Whatever solution your company sells, I can guarantee you it is not rocket science. Be hungry, be curious, and be eager to learn more; start poking around your product by yourself. You will be amazed by how much you can learn off standard training materials.

3. *Your Market and Theirs*: As a subject matter expert, you need to speak your prospect's language, which implies knowing the challenges and opportunities that the markets in which they operate usually bring. As a specialist in your industry, you need to show visionary thinking to establish yourself as an advisor in *their* selection process. Research is key to share knowledge and expertise; explore analyst papers, investigate industry trends, or simply surf the web for industry content and absorb as much knowledge as you can.

4. *Your Competition*: You might not care too much about your competition, but guess what? They know about you. Your goal should be to beat, explain, reject, and react to your competitors' assertions. The best way to kill the competition is to prove them wrong, which is much easier than one would think. But remember, the same applies to you; you could be proven wrong if you provide incorrect information about your competitors' offering. Stay on top of your competitor's moves, positioning, and products, and delicately express your opinion on your competition by never calling them out by name and always inviting your prospect to verify your assessment with the competition directly. Your credibility will go through the roof!

I am sure your company will have on-boarding programs and training campuses you can attend to learn more about the market, the product, the competition, and the company for which you work. These are all great educational events you should take advantage of, but it is not enough. It is on you to want to learn more, and your company website, your competitor's websites, and the internet in general are the best sources of education for you. There is no valid excuse not to be an expert in the industry for which you work, the company you represent, and your direct competition.

True Story – Know Who You Work For!

I once was at a presentation in New York City for an important prospect in the media industry, together with one of my most senior account executives. After the usual set up and introductions, the account executive started with the corporate overview (yes, we all could write numerous books on why *not* to start with the corporate overview) and two minutes into the presentation, the VP of Finance stopped him and asked what our company name meant and where it came from. Given that my company name at that time was not even one of the most intuitive to remember, the embarrassed account executive had to pass the ball on to me and admit he did not know.

KNOW YOUR BASICS	
What to Do	**What Not to Do**
Know your Company's Mission and Values	Wait for instructions
Be an expert at the product you promote	Assume you know enough to get by
Research the market	Show up and throw up
Study the competition	
Practice, rehearse, and practice again	

Working the Demo Cycle

From the moment you get a call from your Sales Rep until the contract is signed, you are on the hook and need to excel every step of the way.

In traditional software sales, the sales process from a Sales Engineer's perspective is made up of the components below. Not all of them might apply within a sales cycle, but this should represent a comprehensive list of potential touchpoints you as a Sales Engineer could be involved with.

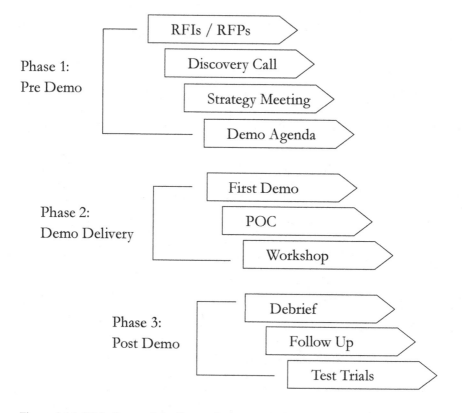

Figure 2.1.1. Main Steps of the Demo Cycle

Chapter 2.2 – Phase 1: Pre Demo

Pre-demo is probably the most important phase of the entire process along with the last one, the post-demo phase. All we are doing in the pre-demo stage is preparing for demo day and building rapport with our prospects. Preparation includes understanding our prospect's business, requirements, and priorities. This can be done in a variety of ways; by responding to tedious Request for Proposals issued by the prospect, jumping on a discovery call to learn more about their objectives, and putting it all together in a well-defined winning strategy. At any touchpoint with our prospective customer during this phase, you will have three objectives in mind:

1. Making it about THEM and not about you or your product

2. Establishing credibility

3. Getting the answers you need

Let's now take a look at what we will be working on in this phase.

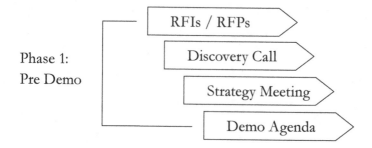

Phase 1:
Pre Demo

Figure 2.2.1. Main Steps of the Pre Demo Phase of the Sales Cycle

Request for Proposal

A request for proposal (RFP) is a sales engineer's nightmare and is typically the first real touchpoint we have with a lead. Usually multiple pages long—with questions that we find trivial, rightfully doubting if anyone will ever read our answers—RFPs represent a very time- and resource-intensive activity of the presales process. This chapter will examine how to convert RFPs from a necessary evil to a competitive advantage, knowing very well they have to be answered if we decide to go ahead with that opportunity.

- Influence the RFP submission: If our account executive is working the deal properly, maybe we have already established a good rapport with the prospect that is about to issue a request for proposal. The beauty of getting involved in a deal before the prospect goes shopping for a solution is that we can influence the way our prospective customers will tackle the selection process. As much as we hate answering those RFPs, customers hate coming up with all the questions. Proposing to help with the RFP write up by sending the prospect past RFPs used for similar opportunities allows us to reduce the length of the sales cycle and, most importantly, it allows us to have input in the questions submitted to all the vendors competing on the opportunity.

- If we are not lucky or creative enough to be in a position to influence the RFP process at all, and we simply get an invitation to bid with a tight deadline, the first thing we have to do is question the qualification of the opportunity and decide whether to respond or not. The decision should be made considering many factors: value (both financial and strategic) of the deal versus the effort required to respond, current workload and future resource availability, deadline, any major functionality or legal requirement that we cannot meet, etc. Reading the RFP is the first step in assessing how much work it will require. Some might have boiler-plate requirements that we have already responded to in past proposals. Others—the most intelligent ones—might instead require some investigation, information gathering, and are time-intensive activities. If all the stars do not align (product fit, resource availability, respect of the timeline, etc.), it is better to either ask for an extension (in case the only problem is meeting the deadline) or decide not to bid at all.

- Once the decision is made to go ahead, the RFP answering process is a team effort coordinated by the account executive. The sales rep is the owner of the account, and he or she will have to make sure the RFP is answered thoroughly by the deadline. Divide and conquer is the mantra for responding to RFPs. Sales account executives are typically in charge of any section asking about your company's background and viability, financial proposal, and customer references. Presales is in charge of everything product-related, which is typically the core and most intensive part of the RFP. IT and Tech Ops are involved in any technical sections of the RFP aiming to evaluate the architecture of your solution, and Professional Services might also be involved to respond to questions related to the implementation and support of the solution after it goes live. It is worth noticing that most established organizations with a considerable RFP activity might hire a Technical Writer as part of the Sales or Presales team. This position is extremely relevant and useful only if the ownership of the RFP still stays with the account executive and the technical writer coordinates with all other stakeholders and Subject Matter Experts (SMEs) to make sure the responses provided are accurate and right to the point. The risk of hiring a Technical Writer to be in charge of RFP responses is the lack of deep domain expertise, which is why it is fundamental for that position to constantly coordinate with other SMEs.

- Establish credibility throughout the RFP process. A well-structured and professionally-edited RFP response goes a long way. This is the first real impression your prospect will be getting of you and the quality of the work you deliver; use them wisely as RFPs represent a great chance for you to set the bar and gain credibility. Avoid boilerplate and copied-and-pasted answers from past RFPs, and instead, make all your answers specific to the customer's requests. Demand clarification (if not already scheduled by the prospective customer) to ask any question you need clarity on to better phrase a response.

- Attend RFP clarification calls organized by the prospect. These quick events are a great way to learn more about your competition while also gaining additional knowledge about your prospective customer and establishing credibility. Most of the time it is not required for you to be informed about your competition when attending the call, but it is easy to infer from the questions being asked who else is bidding together with you, which will greatly help you during the sales cycle.

- Add an executive summary. Even if not expressly requested in the RFP, do add a one-pager on how your products and solutions meet and exceed the customer's requirements, and stress how your company conforms to the customer's vision and mission. I always assume that even the most excruciating RFPs are analyzed at least by whoever puts them together. I doubt the entire team, especially when the decision is a consensual agreement, will read the entire document, but I have to believe the people that developed it in the first place will want to see the fruits of their hard work. For everybody else, including top management, the key is to probate a well-written, polished executive summary that highlights the exact points we want to communicate.

- If your business is very RFP-intensive, consider creating a library of standard answers to frequently asked questions such as your release policy or your support hours. This is typically information that rarely changes and that seldom needs to be "adjusted" for specific customers, considerably reducing the response time. Also, evaluate purchasing an RFP tool. Many solutions in today's market can skim the RFP document independently and suggest responses by extrapolating from past answered RFPs. In any case, it is fundamental to keep your company and product information up to date to avoid submitting answers that are not applicable (product versioning, price list changes, etc.)

True Story: The Power of Subject Matter Expertise

You can avoid RFPs! Not that I have been able to do so every single time, but with 10+ years of experience in an industry with a decent amount of RFP activity, I have been able to skip quite a few. The key is to enter the sales cycle well before the customer has realized its needs and establish yourself as the indisputable subject matter expert (SME). It happened to me recently on an opportunity with a Financial Services organization in Connecticut. This was a previous customer of ours, successfully using our products for something else. I owe it to my marketing department that we were on the top of their needs when they started scouting the market for a new regulatory solution. We visited our customer immediately, fully committed not to have any other vendor penetrate that organization. Right away, we proposed a Requirements Session with our subject matter experts and a full-blown proof of concept (POC) with the agreement that, if they liked what they saw, they would not issue an RFP. Luckily enough, the POC went well and we acquired their business without ever undergoing a formal selection process.

REQUEST FOR PROPOSAL	
What to Do	**What Not to Do**
Influence the RFP write-up	Copy and paste from past RFPs
Assume a "Divide and Conquer" approach	Reference outdated/inconsistent information
Establish credibility throughout the process	Submit poorly written content (typos, etc.)
Add an executive summary	
Consider purchasing an RFP tool	

Discovery Call

A discovery call is probably the most important milestone in any demo preparation yet is one of the most often underrated items. Discovery calls, also known as Needs Analysis, refer to a very delicate moment in the pre-demo phase of any sales cycle where the Sales Engineer meets with the prospect to discuss their requirements, their current challenges, and the vision of their initiative. This is not the place to talk about your company or the products you sell; this is all about THEM and YOU. While requirements gathering might seem the obvious goal of any discovery call, it is probably the least important. Let's face it, chances are that if you are an experienced subject matter expert in your industry, many of the challenges your potential customers will tell you about are not new to you. However, even jumping on the phone with your prospective customer for a quick 30-minute conversation to talk about them has many advantages:

- It shows your prospect you are focusing on THEM and are giving them special attention. Every customer thinks they are special; some of them indeed are—the great majority not so much, but they still deserve your attentiveness. Everybody likes to feel appreciated and this the right time to give your prospects your utmost consideration by listening to them and making them realize you care about their vision and priorities.

- It allows you to understand more about their business and their common frustrations. By asking questions about how they do things today and what improvements they want to achieve, you will acquire valuable knowledge to leverage during your presentation. Show them what they want to see and not what you are proud of. The discovery call in its most brutal sense does exactly that: it enables you to focus your presentation on the key areas the customer wants to improve rather than blindly show your product for two hours straight.

- It builds rapport and adds to the credibility you must constantly develop and strengthen during the entire sales cycle. By talking to them about their challenges and objectives, you can use the experience you have gained with other customers that had similar issues and provide a different angle or perspective. Without sounding arrogant or lecturing them on how they should be running their business, this is the chance for you to set yourself as an unbiased advisor to whom your prospects will enjoy talking.

- It allows you to learn more than they would be willing to disclose to your sales reps—the old saying "people buy from people" could not be more true. By focusing on them, your prospects will be inclined to share more with you and listen to you. This will give you a chance to influence their requirements towards those areas your company and products shine the best or better understand their internal decisional process.

- Finish your call by asking the prospect to acknowledge what problems or processes they want the new solution to fix and what their top priorities are for the upcoming initiative. These will be the opening points of your live demo.

It is evident that discovery calls are extremely valuable and represent a not-to-be-missed milestone of any sales cycle. First impressions usually make for a long-lasting impact; use the discovery call to impress your prospects.

What if your prospect does not want to take the call?

Well, it is your sales rep's job to make it happen: he or she will have to work some magic and get their prospect to your discovery call. It is in your sales rep's best interest that a discovery call is booked on your calendar. If you are told your prospect is not willing to jump on any pre-demo call with you, chances are your prospect has already made a decision and is only trying to tick a box in their evaluation checklist.

Recommendation:

Create a standardized "Discovery Cheat Sheet" for all your needs-analysis meetings and run your calls in a way to get as many answers to your questions as you can. By having a checklist handy with some key questions bolded, it will ensure you get the minimum information you need to be effective on your next demo. Taking it to the next level, have your marketing team convert your "Cheat Sheet" into a professionally-designed document and send it to all of those prospects claiming they do not have time to jump on a 30-minute discovery call.

DISCOVERY CALL	
What to Do	**What Not to Do**
Listen, Process, and Learn	Simply take notes
Demonstrate industry experience	Focus on today's challenges only
Drive questions with storytelling	Ask too many questions
Uncover problems	Have the AE run the call on your behalf
Build relationships and trust	Be "selly"

Strategy Meeting

We have all the info we can think of to start strategizing on how we want to approach this new opportunity. Strategy definition is a team effort and involves a leader and multiple contributors. The leader is your account executive in charge of the opportunity; he or she owns the deal and has to define the action plan to successfully close the sale. A valid deal strategy plan should not simply dictate what needs to be done, by whom, and when—that is a tactical plan; it should rather highlight what to do to set yourself apart from the competition. Strategizing before the demo involves considering the following:

- Meeting Goal and MAAP (Mutually Agreed Action Plan): What do we want to accomplish with this meeting, and how does this meeting fit in the overall sales cycle? What is the MAAP with the prospect? What happens after this presentation?

- Customer Stories and References: What customers of ours should we mention during the meeting with similar challenges? What case studies should we include in our presentation? Did any of our customers dismiss our competitor's products and solutions for ours? Why?

- Partners: Do we need sponsorship from the partner channel? Are any of our current partners already involved with that prospect somehow? Can we join forces with any of our partners to gain credibility and trustworthiness?

- Competition: How should we attack our competitors during the presentation? How open and direct do we want to be? What traps should we lay to make it harder for our competitors? What can we anticipate the competition will say about us?

- Audience: What is the "political map" within the decision makers? Who are our key players, influencers, detractors, and promoters? Who should we focus on? Who does the prospect's CEO go golfing with on the weekends? What company did the decision makers work for in the past?

- Executive Commitment: Do we need our top management to support us and show executive sponsorship? Do we need our CEO to maybe drop a quick email to our prospect's selection committee?

- Additional Help: Do we need help from anybody else in the organization? Do we need the sales ops to arm us with relevant collaterals, statistics, research papers, or any other assets that could be relevant for our prospect? Do we need marketing to run specific email campaigns to a set of decision makers with a tailored message? Do we need Professional Services to join the meeting and showcase their expertise with the prospects' requirements? Do we need product management to tag along, disclose our roadmap, and commit to future developments?

- Value Statement: The value statement is the most important of all. As a team, you will have to decide the top two or three items are on which your entire presentation will focus. Those items will be what your account executive will position at the very beginning, will be reinforced by your solution demo, and will be validated by the stories you will be telling. This is the time you all agree on what VALUE your solution will bring to your prospective customer and how the entire presentation should be structured around that. Ask yourself the question: "Why should this company buy our solution?"

The key to a Strategy meeting is to start thinking PROACTIVELY. The worst thing to do is think there is nothing else to do and that we have done everything we could ever do.

On planes, the pilot's typical line is "sit back, relax, and enjoy the ride."

In Sales, my line is "Stand up, get going, and call your prospect."

 **Recommendation:**

Request a Strategy Meeting. Of course not all the opportunities you will be involved with will require the participation of your channel, marketing, and product management teams, but for those high-value deals (of both financial and/or strategic value), it is imperative to coordinate and proactively think about what to do. My experience has taught me that even if this is in the best interest of any account executive, sometimes they are too busy prospecting that they forget what is right there on their plate. Be adamant about it and invite your sales reps to take action and schedule a strategy call for you and them to lay out the path to success. Do not be afraid to look like a bothering pest; you are helping them succeed. If they win that business, you win as well!

STRATEGY MEETING	
What to Do	**What Not to Do**
Call a strategy meeting	Sit back, relax, and enjoy the ride
Think outside of the box	Think there is nothing else to do
Be proactive	
Ask yourself what, why, and for whom	
Challenge your account executive	

Demo Agenda

Now that you know your prospective customer's vision and requirements for the initiative you have been called to consult on, and you have also debriefed with your account executive on what strategy to adopt, it is time to package that information in a flow that best fits your solution and your prospect's priorities. Draft your agenda in a way to present a story—one that tells how your solution addresses your customer's needs and what value it brings to them. Close it up with a clear recap of how your solution brings value to their business in a very factual approach. Your demo agenda:

- Needs to be put together by you, the Demo Guru, not the sales rep. Do not have your sales rep send any product-specific agenda or flow. You are in control of the product section of the meeting, and you dictate how it will flow.

- Needs to be sent to your prospect before the presentation. This is a key step to make sure you have buy-in from your prospective customer. Send the agenda to your champion or have the sales rep send it; you need to get your prospect's feedback on what you plan on showing before demo day.

- Should focus on the customer's needs and the value your solution will bring to them rather than presenting a set of 30 bullet points mentioning each feature and function you will be showing. Draft your agenda in a way to properly address the business need and keep it concise and to the point. I like my demo agenda flow to have two slides: one that lists my understanding of their main issues, and one with how I am planning to solve them with my solution.

- Should be an extremely safe practice for all of your new sales engineers who might not be experts with your solutions yet. Compiling, and most importantly sharing, the agenda with your sponsor delineates the perimeter you will be working in with fewer unexpected items that could expose your limited experience with the solution you are proposing.

- Is only a guide to help you control the meeting; by no means should it be set in stone nor should it represent the only areas with which you are comfortable. Be ready to go off script, move your demo items around, drop any topic that your audience is not too interested in, and add new ones depending on the temperature of the room.

During your presentation, start by clearly stating the two major requirements you have learned from your past calls with the prospect. This will show everybody in the room—not only those few people you had the discovery call with—that you have done your homework and you are going to get right to the point. This will also give you the opportunity to make sure you have not missed anybody's requests or concerns. Once everybody knows you are aware of their main objectives, walk them through how you'll address them by quickly skimming through your agenda items, making it very clear that it is just for guidance and that you will be thrilled to address any off-agenda topic. Giving your audience visibility into what is coming will give them reassurance that you will at some point get to what each of them cares the most about in that meeting.

 **Recommendation:**

When reviewing your agenda during the presentation, always have an empty line at the bottom. That empty line will be the topic you will be asking your audience to add on the fly in case you have missed anything. This will not only show you already know about their business requirements and overall objectives but will convey how flexible and confident you are that your solution will meet any impromptu new requirement they might have.

DEMO AGENDA	
What to Do	**What Not to Do**
Share it with your sponsor beforehand	Mention every single feature you will show
Start with your take on the AS-IS situation	Talk too long about each component
Encourage your audience to add more	Ignore prospect's new additions
Walk your audience through what is coming	Have your sales rep write it
Add a recap slide focused on value proposition	

 **Extra Tip!**

Ask for a Demo Dry Run. We will cover later what a Dry Run Demo is, but this type of software presentation is extremely helpful to validate the agenda not only on paper but also in action! Any additional touch point with your key stakeholders will allow you to build rapport, establish credibility and continuously learn more about their needs and mindset.

Chapter 2.3 – Phase 2: Demo Delivery

We are finally on! We have spent so many hours responding to our prospect's RFP (and probably just as many doubting they will ever read it) and have engaged with them during our discovery call. We got their buy-in on what we plan on showing and even confirmed it live with our sponsor. It is now our turn to start sharing our screen. This chapter will illustrate the many different flavors a demonstration could have depending on where we stand in the sales cycle and the actual qualification of the prospect to whom we are about to demo.

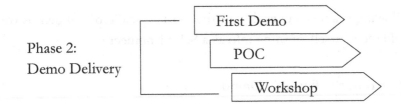

Figure 2.3.1. Main Steps of the Demo Delivery Phase of the Sales Cycle

No matter what type of demo you present, some basic behaviors and generic principles always apply. Before showing up for a demo, it is mandatory to know the type of audience you will be talking to (decision makers, influencers, sponsors, hostile users, etc.)

Whether you are demoing first, last, or somewhere in between, adopting a different strategy depending on your turn in the prospects' evaluation process is of utmost importance. Knowing your competition is a must; you may not know *exactly* who your opponent is, but understanding what the prospect liked or disliked about the competition is a huge help.

Also, refer to upcoming chapters on how to engage with your audience and presales best practices to make sure you are as effective as possible in any circumstance.

<u>Demo Types</u>

There is a demo for every occasion!

Presales is usually called to show the product in a variety of circumstances. The marketing department is planning a booth at an industry conference and we need to show our product. We have been shortlisted with our main competitor and we are now on for a final bake-off demo, or we are simply helping our lead generation team to spread the word about our offering with a webinar. Every occasion has specific goals and objectives, and the approach we should follow for demoing our services and products should be different and in line with the overall strategy of the meeting.

Following is a quick overview of the most typical types of demos you could see yourself running into as a Sales Engineer.

The Art of the Possible Demo

I am borrowing this term from a sales rep with whom I previously worked. I hate this term as it goes against everything we have discussed so far: deal qualification. This specific demo type is also usually referred to as the "gatekeeper demo," and guess what? It is *not* a demo.

This is just a get together with the prospect where we let them be completely in charge of the sales cycle. Being asked to show "a bit of everything" in an hour or so is wholly inefficient and a waste of time for any experienced Sales Engineer. The total lack of qualification could instead have a counter effect that makes the whole situation worse.

Not knowing what the prospect is looking for could result in showing a variety of disconnected screens that do not resonate with the prospect, risking elimination from the selection process before even beginning.

The best way to avoid these types of demos is of course to have our sales mates explain to the prospective customers the little value they will get from such a generic demonstration. Sometimes our sales counterparts do not want to push back or have this type of conversation with their prospective customer, claiming we will be eliminated if we do not show up. At other times, introductory demos are a necessary evil given the prospect's stubbornness and there is little that can be done. In such cases, we as Demo Gurus have no other choice than to surrender and start demoing.

There are, however, a few options to limit the involvement of the most experienced sales engineers (the people sales reps would like to have on any single deal) in the Art of the Possible Demos.

- First, having weekly generic webinars as part of your marketing plan could help tremendously. These could be either live webinars led by less experienced sales engineers given their scripted nature. These live events, or maybe pre-recorded events, potentially could be even sent on demand to the prospect.

- As an alternative, create a set of pre-recorded videos, nothing too fancy or "selly," that focus on a very specific aspect of your solution. Having a gallery of quick product snippets that you could even publish on your website would be extremely helpful to bypass many gatekeeper demos. I experienced this myself.

At my current company, we now have a library of more than 40 two-minute demos that have been recorded by my Presales team. Our sales reps love those assets and constantly send them to prospects of ours that are just scouting the market for more info.

- If your solution and products allow, have your sales reps run these introductory Art of the Possible Demos. The level of technical knowledge of these types of demos is very low, and usually following a script with some color commentary does the job. Even if your sales rep is not the best technical presenter, he or she should be able to get the job done, making it easier for you to shine even brighter when you give the main presentation.

True Story: A Rookie Mistake

This happened to me a few years back during a demonstration I was conducting at a publishing company in the Boston area. I received a call on my cell from one of my sales reps. Apparently, this prospect was evaluating vendors already, and if we did not do a demo the next day to the VP of Finance, we would be out of the deal. When I asked what they wanted to see in the demo, my sales rep said: "Everything. Show them everything because they do not know better." Not knowing better myself, I agreed to do the demo the next day. By then, my background was mostly around automating cash flow planning processes—basically translating profit and loss budgets into cash flow projections. What little I knew ten years ago! The following day I logged in to my web demo and started talking about how powerful our solution was at generating fully balanced cash flow projections in a matter of seconds. A couple of minutes into the presentation, the VP of Finance interrupted and clarified, "We are not at all interested in automating cash flows as that is done by a different team. We are interested in seeing how you can help us with our development spending." It goes without saying we had to stop the demo and convert that meeting into a discovery call. We then went back, demonstrated what they wanted to see, and acquired their business.

Top 3 Takeaways:

	The ART OF THE POSSIBLE Demo
#1	Stay away from these types of presentations as their generic nature may not speak to the exact needs and pains your audience is trying to address.
#2	Collaborate with your counterpart in Sales to explain your prospective customers the little value they will be getting from these types of presentations.
#3	Leverage marketing assets such as weekly webinars or pre-recorded product videos to share with your audience as an introduction to your solution with the goal of conducting a more focused and tailored demonstration at a later time.

The Standard Demo

There should not be such a thing as "Standard Demos."

Also referred to as "Canned Demos," standard demos are generic presentations that do not tailor our products and solutions to the needs and profile of the audience to whom we are talking. These generic presentations lack power and effectiveness and are hard to digest for prospects who constantly have to connect the dots between what is presented to them and how the generic demo example reflects the current problems within their company.

Standard demos also inevitably force you to compete in a "beauty contest," where all is focused on the look and feel of the solution versus its depth of functionality.

Even though we want to stay away from standard product tours that could be easily achieved by sending the recording of a past webinar, standard demos play, however, a fair part in the following cases, which, as you will realize, will serve more as a benefit for YOU than your prospect:

- During Onboarding: Any new hire needs to start somewhere, and providing a standard, guided demo flow together with a script will allow the new sales engineers to practice and learn the basics of your products and solutions.

- For Lead Generation Webinars: Very often, presales is involved in lead generation activities, such as weekly product webinars, that our marketing department promotes across multiple regions and industries. Usually, registrants come from different profiles and many different fields, making it impossible to tailor the demonstration in any specific way. These webinars are generic and have the goal of "intriguing" your audience and inviting them to know more. The all-encompassing nature of this type of demos requires focusing on your solution's most-asked features, main differentiation points, and most demonstrable value it brings to its users.

- As a safety net for questions that might come up for which you have not been able to customize your demo assets. Relying on a comprehensive demo package that includes most use cases, even if generic, would allow you to refer to them in case the prospect is adamant about having a specific requirement not included in the original discussions demonstrated at any cost.

Recognizing that sometimes standard demos are necessary beyond the areas described above, the sales engineer should still strive to make the demo more personal for the prospect and speak their language. If the solution or product you are demoing allows, try to apply some "cheesy" demo alterations that usually go a long way with your audience:

- Add your prospects' logo and branding on the homepage of your software solution. I have never really been too fond of this minimal level of customization as it almost shows a lack of interest in trying anything else, but at least for some potential buyers, this technique will still get you some points.

- Rename your standard demo assets to match your prospect's business and industry. If you are presenting your standard hotel-booking demo case to a restaurant-booking provider, you might want to change the names of your standard demo hotels into the restaurants your prospective customer currently serves.

- Change the color scheme of your application to match the experience, look, and feel of your customer's website.

- Get rid of your generic demo user *"DEMO1"* and create a demo user with the name of one of the team members of the prospect to whom you are demoing.

- Update your demo data! Stop showing KPIs saying *"2004 vs 2005 ROS"*—it screams laziness and shows you pay little attention to details.

Depending on the product you are demoing, these quick tricks will show your prospect you took the time to genuinely think about them and make it easier for them to follow. They might not like your solution at the end of the day, but they will appreciate the effort!

 **Recommendation:**

For the great majority of my work life, I have been demoing to Finance and Accounting folks. I think it is fair to say that accountants are not necessarily known for their enthusiasm and passion, neither are they typically adamant about change. Imagine showing a solution that will disrupt their routines and get them out of their comfort zone. Even with my last second demos, I always try to make it easier for them to follow. By visiting their website, you can change your dashboards to include the locations in which they do business. Look at their public filings; you can make a simple report look just like one they always consult. If your product is as good as mine is, this will take you minutes with a guaranteed *"Thank you for taking the time to re-build our reports with your solution"* at the end of the presentation.

Top 3 Takeaways:

The STANDARD Demo	
#1	Is hard for prospective customers to digest as standard demos require a lot of effort on the customer's side to translate how the generic demo use case might be applicable to their own specific business needs.
#2	Should be limited in use to only wide and diversified audiences such as in the case of webinars, conference presentations, or as a back-up for unexpected questions.
#3	Should always rely on updated demo assets with basic modifications to include your prospect's logo, color scheme, and products or locations by simply visiting their website.

The Custom Demo

This should be your GO-TO TYPE of demo. You have the moral responsibility to take all of the knowledge you acquired during the pre-demo phase—responding to the RFPs, being on multiple calls with the prospect, etc.—to fruition. Custom Demos do exactly that: they capitalize on the information you have acquired by talking to your prospect.

Custom demos are not to be confused with Proof of Concepts or Test Trials (more on both later). Custom demos take your standard demo assets to the next level by positioning and enhancing them in a way they instantly resonate with your prospect and immediately show value for them.

With custom demos:

- Always include some examples of specific requirements that have been discussed in previous interactions to show how your customer's current needs could be addressed and enhanced in your solution. Without running into a full implementation, custom demos aim to include basic customizations of your standard demo assets in your presentation even without being openly asked.

- Start at the end, focusing on the expected results they hope to achieve by purchasing a new solution. Showing the outcome before walking them through in-depth product details has many advantages: it shows your solution can deliver on their main goals, creating a sense of reassurance in the room, and it ignites a sense of awe and curiosity to see how you got to the finished product. You now have their attention.

- Quickly address the "me too" to make sure we are not forgetting the basics! The risk of tailoring the entire demo to the prospects' specific requirements is that you might not be showing some basic functionality that instead they have seen in prior demonstrations from our competitors. This could leave your prospect with the feeling that your solution is not "up to par" with the other solutions in the market. Right after your WOW intro, slow down a bit and make sure you hit all of the common checks they would expect a solution like yours to have. This will serve as peace of mind for your audience to know your solution is, at a minimum, like all the others they have seen and will simultaneously allow you to gauge your audience and understand their level of sophistication.

- Go back into full "custom mode" and hit hard on their pain points again. This is the time for you to spruce up your flow again and start talking about the challenges of their current situation. Focus on one specific pain point they have been very adamant about in your prior conversations, and show them how your solution will fix it. Use your product as a launching pad to show, but mostly explain, the value your solution will bring to them. This is when you talk about how other customers are facing the same challenge, highlight the risks of the current approach, and start exposing your competition. Your product, your voice, the experience you bring to the table, the way you make eye-contact with your audience, and the screens you share all have to work harmoniously in this phase to win your prospect over.

- Open their eyes: You probably have demonstrated that your product is a valid candidate for their current business issues by now. Play the visionary card and show them how your solution can help them with more than what they are looking to do now. Even if you are dealing with a very basic product, there is always a different way to look at things without stretching your product's capability.

- End with a close: "Thanks for taking the time to learn about our solution today, I really appreciate it. I hope this has been informative for you, and if you have any further questions at any time, just let me know." This is not an effective close. Close by bringing up the slide deck you used at the beginning of the presentation and focus on their two top priorities again. Quickly recap how your solution will address those priorities by reminding them of the functionality you discussed earlier until you see the first nod in the room. That is the sign your recap is over and it's now time for the account executive to wrap it up by asking the infamous question, "How did we do?"

True Story: European Style in North America

Demoing style varies a lot by country, and you need to consider the culture of the audience to whom you are demoing. When I initially came to the US after many years in Europe, where I was first exposed to demonstrations, I was completely ignorant of the demonstration style on this side of the pond and kept demoing in my own, European way. My first 50 minutes were usually a personal monologue on how to configure our product, and I proudly even used to show the least known flags of our application. It took me quite a bit to understand I was training my prospects instead of showing them the way to succeed.

 Top 3 Takeaways:

The CUSTOM Demo	
#1	Tailors your standard demo assets to support the information gathered during you discovery phase to hit exactly on what your prospects value the most.
#2	Still addresses both basic functionality that is standard to make sure your solution levels with your competitors' and also highlights unsolicited requirements.
#3	Is not to be confused with a Proof of Concept or Training session.

The Keynote Demo

I love this type of demonstration. They give me so much positive anxiety, and by now I have learned to translate it into adrenaline and excitement. Keynote demos are those quick 5-10 minute demonstrations that you are called to do at User Conference or Product Launch events, usually in a plenary session, side-by-side with your company CEO, and typically in front of hundreds or thousands of people.

It's usually not the huge audience that creates anxiety for these types of events, nor is it the fact that you have your CEO's undivided attention being right there with you—you've been there before as an experienced Sales Engineer. It is typically the technology you are about to demo that gives you the chills.

Rightfully so, these events focus on the latest and greatest of your product offering, quite often even providing sneak peeks into what is coming next. That, by definition, is NOT stable, hence why you get the chills. The night before, development passes you the latest version of the solution you will have to demo, using scary terms like "latest trunk" or "alpha version," and tells you not to touch anything else. On top of that, your marketing department wants everything to connect wirelessly because cables do not show well on stage.

So you see why the key here is to transform your anxiety into genuine adrenaline and your adrenaline into ultimate fulfillment. When you are done with those 7-10 minutes, which to you seemed to last only two seconds, the gratification at the end is incommensurable. The key to these types of demos is controlling your emotions.

Your demo flow will be successful; you have rehearsed your clicks countless times, and you've been given a dedicated wireless connection by the audio and visual crew that no one is using but you. Everything will work, technologically speaking. Just be sure to control your feelings backstage and let the adrenaline explode when your name is called to go on stage. Now all you can do is to enjoy the moment.

 **Recommendation:**

Find your own way to gain control of your emotions. There are many classes and techniques that explain and teach how to control your feelings, even making the most out of them by converting fear, anxiety, and nervousness into positive energy. Everybody is different, and the human mind has its own unique logic; what might work for one individual might not work for another. One thing is sure, though: transform whatever emotion you might be experiencing the seconds before going on stage into adrenaline. Adrenaline is what you need to master Keynote Demos. Personally, I use a very cheap method made of process and people. From a process perspective, I practice my intro words to death; I feel that if my intro is spot on in terms of words, tone, energy, pace, and passion, the rest will come. I also always prepare a few back-up lines in case anything goes wrong and the demo cannot be performed or crashes unexpectedly.

From a people standpoint, I ask my go-to IT Guru (yes, Demo Gurus have their favorite IT mates) to be there off stage with me just in case anything happens before or during my 10 minutes of glory.

Thank you, IT!

 Top 3 Takeaways:

The KEYNOTE Demo	
#1	Aims to impress and excite a wide audience usually at larger gatherings such as Product Launches or User Conferences.
#2	Requires a "Plan B" approach in case anything goes wrong during the live demonstration.
#3	Demands high control of emotions to translate anxiety into adrenaline.

The Web Demo

The peculiar aspect of Web Demos is how they are delivered rather than their content. You could perform standard, custom, or differentiation demos all via the web, but I decided to isolate this ever-rising breed, as specific attention needs to be focused on web demos. The recent global pandemic has dramatically increased the popularity of this type of demo given the social distancing requirements we all have been instructed to follow. Most importantly, it has proven that buyers can still make decisions off of Web demonstrations.

Just like the name suggests, these presentations are completely or mostly remote demonstrations. More times than not, both the sales engineer and the account executive are connecting remotely; other times, the sales rep might go onsite to the customer's location while the presales resource prefers avoiding the travel to spend more time preparing.

No matter what the scenario is, the demonstration will be performed via the web, meaning you will not be able to see your audience's reactions, even with the greatest screen-sharing technology available. The benefits of web demos are obvious: you can reach more people at once, you can keep your sales costs low, and you can invest the time you otherwise would be spending on travel into more revenue-generating activities.

The real question to understand is this: When is a web demo a viable option to consider, and how do you mitigate its inherent risks?

Not all types of presentations and meetings are adequate for web delivery:

- Complicated sessions that involve extensive explanations, white-boarding sessions, and Q&A brainstorming are preferred to be run onsite

- Longer presentations that span over multiple hours are not recommended to be performed on the web as it is easier for your audience to lose attention. If that is the only option, try to break out your web demo in multiple 90-minute sessions and plan for frequent breaks

- Any session requiring hands-on participation from your audience is not recommended to be run on the web, even in today's world where many webcasting solutions do offer screen control on top of typical screen sharing.

Conversely, some situations fit perfectly for web demos:

- Introductory, first standard demos that require mostly showing and telling rather than actively engaging your audience in extensive discussions and brainstorming sessions

- Follow up sessions to revisit items that were left out from prior onsite presentations, such as touchpoints on specific, well-defined areas of interest, etc.

- In a situation where you have a very desperate, multinational attendance pool that would be otherwise challenging to meet physically.

No matter what the reason is, when opting for Web Demos, the most challenging aspect is gauging your audience's level of attention, interest, and involvement in what you are showing. In other words, it is hard to read the room and understand how you are doing.

Use the following tricks to engage your audience and test their level of participation:

- Show your face! It might sound embarrassing at first, but the recent global health occurrences have taught us that human beings can tolerate physical distancing but have a hard time tolerating social distancing. Showing your face also generates attention: people are naturally curious, if not nosy, to see what you look like! It would be best to use any screen sharing device that will allow you to turn your camera on. You do not need to run a two-hour demo showing your face, but I do strongly recommend activating your camera during introductions and show yourself! Then, you can de-activate it for the bulk of the presentation, resuming a live show maybe at the end or during breaks. If live camera is not your thing, try at least to have the first slide with a picture of yourself and anyone presenting from your team (Sales Rep, SME, etc.) Use that slide at the very beginning when your team is being introduced to the prospect. Make it personal even if you are distant!

- If possible, ask your audience to introduce themselves and express their objectives for the meeting. During your demonstration, circle back to what you have learned during the intro and openly call out how the feature you are about to show meets Susan's requirement she expressed in her intro. Tying back demo items to personal objectives is crucial in web demos to keep your audience engaged.

- Avoid asking generic questions like, *"Does anyone have any questions so far?"* It is almost guaranteed to evoke no response. Use more of a polling approach where you address your audience by name. This will make your session more personal and will counterbalance the lack of "human rapport" a web demo intrinsically implies.

- A lively demo flow coupled with a captivating tone and pace are vital aspects to keep your audience engaged in web demos. Avoid the standard typical presentation flow of corporate overview first, then product demo for the remainder of the session, and a Q&A slide to wrap it up. Break your demo flow into chunks where you combine 10-12 minutes of product demonstration, followed by a 1-2 minute recap slide, and then open it up for Q&A right away before moving to the next item. This will make sure you are not talking to yourself for 45 minutes straight, and you are forcing your audience to pay attention. See the extra tip at the end of this chapter to incorporate Quiz Questions throughout your presentation to keep the audience engaged.

Top 3 Takeaways:

The WEB Demo	
#1	Is not a good fit for the most complex and lengthy demonstrations with wider audiences that might also require hands-on participation.
#2	Presents difficulties to the presenter to "read the room" and assess how the audience is receiving the demonstration, especially if not particularly active.
#3	Requires the presenter to keep the audience's attention high by breaking the demonstration is smaller chunks and leveraging a more "personal" approach to engage with the customer, such as addressing listeners by name, showing your face, polling the audience, etc.

The Tradeshow Demo

These demos certainly prove your ability to summarize! These types of demos are quick presentations you will have to give passersby at a conference or tradeshow where your marketing department has rented out a booth and a monitor for you to babysit. You will probably be standing by the booth, most of the time with a self-running video projecting on your monitor. During session breaks, conference attendees coming by to ask questions and take a free gadget will, hopefully, inundate you.

The key to these demos is to master your pitch. You will be asked many times what your product does *("tell me about your product"* is the preferred line of conferences attendees as they reach out for the colored spinner to take home), and you have only a few seconds to make all of the relevant and differentiating points before kicking the ball back in their court.

No demo yet.

There are thousands of books on how to deliver the perfect sales pitch, but in essence, when at a tradeshow, be ready to articulate a concise value proposition about your offering that:

- Is brief and short. I am saying, very short. 45-50 seconds is the right duration of a tradeshow pitch as the attention span of your passersby is shorter than that of a person sitting at a desk in the office mentally prepared to listen to you.

- Includes three main areas: who your company is, what your product does, and how it is different than the competition.

- Leverages effective body language that reflects your engaging tone of voice.

The goal of your tradeshow pitch is to politely answer the question you've been asked right away and engage back with your "passerby" as soon as possible by asking what he or she is interested in. Have them talk and tell you about what they are looking for. Qualify your opportunity. Make it about them, not about you.

Now you can demo.

With the little info you have gathered, including the attendee's title and industry, which are usually available on their conference badges, you have a good idea of whether this individual is just "kicking tire," or if there is some real interest.

If you decide to demo, keep it brief and right to the point. You have to make sure you pick the right functionality and correct screens to impress your user. Mastering your demo assets is vital in Tradeshow Demos given the out-of-the-blue requests you might have. One or two screens, accompanied by a factual customer story over a 5-minute presentation, is all you need at this stage.

Offer your audience a more detailed demo some other time during the conference or when he/she is back at the office. Do not overwhelm your audience with what you want them to see; resist the temptation. Intrigue your audience, create interest, and push it back to a later time when you know more about them.

Make sure you ask for a business card!

 Top 3 Takeaways:

The TRADESHOW Demo	
#1	Requires perfecting your positioning pitch given the limited attention span of conference attendees passing by your booth.
#2	Is usually preceded by a quick "on-the-fly" needs analysis in the form of a casual conversation between the Demo Guru and the conference attendee aiming to unveil what they are looking for more specifically.
#3	Focuses on the main areas briefly discussed with the conference attendee and is kept short on purpose with the goal of suggesting a more detailed presentation at a different time.

The Release Readiness Demo

Typical of the software industry, this type of demo aims to show the latest and greatest product functionality on which our development team has worked. It is good practice for any software provider to communicate what changes and enhancements will be released with the upcoming version and also inform current users of any deprecated feature.

Release Readiness Demos target all internal employees consulting customers on your solutions, your partner network reselling your product, and of course your customer base currently utilizing your software solution. Very rarely do these demos involve prospective customers.

One could argue why presales has to be involved with these types of demos and why instead they are not in charge of product development. The answer is very easy: the potential these demos could bring for additional cross-selling into your customer base is huge, and sales engineers are the most adequate resources to support the technical sale.

During a Release Readiness Demo:

- Focus on the major additions, enhancements, or deprecations that are included in your now Generally Available release. There is no need to mention every minor functionality that was impacted in the release; this will be covered by the Release Notes that should accompany every new version of your software solutions.

- Include a demo of the new features that are being released. It is surprising how many of these new release announcements are merely a tour of fancy, never-ending PowerPoint slides. If possible, use some kind of presentation tool to introduce the new topic, potentially explaining the value this new functionality will bring to the customer base and the originating logic (new market trends or technology, popular requests from the customer base, the internal vision of the product development team, etc.) However, make sure to translate that narrative description of the new feature into an effective three-to-five-minute product demo.

- Give a quick sneak peek into the future product roadmap by having the head of product development participate towards the end of the presentation. This will reassure your customers that the product they acquired is constantly evolving and will be able to support them as their business grows.

- Include a survey as a follow-up to your Release Readiness Webcast. These demos will probably be some of the most attended events with the potential of reaching the majority of your customer base. Many webcasting tools allow polling your attendees either during or at the end of the meeting. I would recommend adding a quick one-minute survey at the end of your presentation where attendees are called to provide feedback on the usability of the new features released and their top requests for any upcoming release. This will allow your product development team to better plan their roadmap and be as responsive as they can to their customers' requests.

 **Recommendation:**

Many of my peers often ask me if Release Readiness Webcasts should be open to prospective customers as well. The answer undoubtedly varies depending on your product, solution, and the stage of the prospective customers in the sales cycle. In the world of software solutions, I do not recommend having your prospective customer participate in any new release update. These events assume some basic knowledge of your solution to fully appreciate the importance and the value of the new features being announced. If not properly contextualized, these announcements could expose new functionality that in reality, the competition has leveraged for a long time already. This could give your prospective customers the idea that your solution is catching up with other more mature products in the market while it might simply be a strategic roadmap decision.

Top 3 Takeaways:

The RELEASE READINESS Demo	
#1	Focuses on "the latest and greatest" functionality delivered by our colleagues in Product Management and Development.
#2	Represents a huge opportunity for additional cross-selling and up-selling into the existing customer base.
#3	Should always include a live demo of the newer functionality and a sneak peek into the future product roadmap.

The Dry Run Demo

This is a crucial step in the sales cycle. Dry Run Demos are presentations that focus on showing the solution—and any customization applied to meet the specific prospect's requirements—to your sponsor well before you give the official presentation to the extended audience.

Not being an official presentation does not imply less preparation; these types of demos constitute an additional touchpoint with your prospects who will appreciate the dedication and the attention you are offering to their initiative.

Dry Run Demos help you:

- Confirm your understanding of the prospect's requirements and get honest and unbiased feedback on the many hours of work you have spent so far customizing your solution and preparing for the "big meeting."

- Practice in a semi-real situation, giving you the ability to rehearse, perfect, and refine your positioning points based on your sponsor's feedback, allowing you to also prepare how to manage your time properly during the main presentation.

- Continue to build rapport with your prospects and confirm, once again, your role of subject matter expert and business advisor who understands the complexity of their business.

- Smooth out any technical issues that might occur on the day of the presentation. Especially for web-demos, make sure your prospective customer can easily connect to your screen-sharing device. Sometimes online desktop-sharing providers require plug-in installations that your prospective customers might not have the administrative rights to install on their workstations. To avoid unnecessary scrambling, make sure everybody can connect before the day of your "big demo."

You will be surprised by how much you will learn from these types of presentations.

Besides the items described above, if properly scheduled after your competition has already presented their solutions, the limited audience on which Dry Run Demos typically rely will make your sponsor feel less formal and potentially share feedback or guide you with your upcoming presentation.

Use this touchpoint as a way to learn more about what they liked or disliked about the competition, to obtain comments and feedback attendees had on prior presentations, or simply to dig for that "wow factor" you will unconditionally have to include in your flow.

The consultative approach to these types of presentations will emotionally lead your project sponsor to be more open and transparent with you.

 Top 3 Takeaways:

The DRY RUN Demo	
#1	Requires as much preparation as any official demonstration, even if the audience is limited in size.
#2	Allows the Demo Guru to confirm his/her understanding or the customer's needs and priorities while building rapport with the buyer.
#3	Presents an opportunity for the Demo Guru to learn more how the customer's team reacted to prior competitive presentations.

The Differentiation Demo

These are not easy demos, but they are extremely effective. These are the presentations where you specifically demo how your solution works better than your competition, and why your competitor's product is inferior.

This type of demo requires two factors to be effective: they have to be positioned at the right time, and you have to be sure what you are saying about your competitors.

Suggest a Differentiation Demo when you know you have been shortlisted together with one other vendor only, AND only, if you feel you are not undoubtedly in the first place. Resorting to these demos when the prospect has not yet finalized its main preferences could result in a waste of time due to the lack of focus. Similarly, given the obvious risk they represent, stay away from them if you feel the competition can beat you or you are leading the evaluation. Your competitor will be asked to do the same you are doing.

Preparing a Differentiation Demo is a very intensive task. First, list out those areas the customer seems most interested in and rate your offering against the competition; identify only a couple of items to focus on. If your product objectively does a better job on all of those points than your competitor's product, then you have an easy task ahead of you. Simply prepare your demo to articulate and factually prove how your solution is superior.

Supposing you do not have access to your competitor's products, research the internet for recent videos, blogs, user communities, or socials postings, and most importantly, your competitor's user manual. Bring that evidence to your meeting and have your prospect ask the competition to prove specific use cases you have highlighted for them.

Do not forget to add off-product items in your Differentiation Demo; focus on aspects such as company stability, partner network, customer and analyst ratings, vision, geo presence, customer satisfaction, etc. as these areas could unveil important red-flags to your prospects.

 **Recommendation:**

Avoid being too ruthless about your competition in your conversation, even if you may feel this type of situation implies that. Remember, you are an advisor to your prospective customers: be professional and respectful of other products and solutions, clearly stating that it is only your understanding of how the competition works—hence why they have to double-check directly with the other vendor. This will make your audience feel wary of what the competition says about your solution and will encourage them to confirm with you.

True Story: My GM Studying Our Competitor's User Manual

My company got invited to demonstrate to a reasonably large organization in the US a few years back. After the first demo, we learned we were not the only one that received the invitation; together with us, 12 other vendors were competing for the same business. Through a very diligent selection process that took a few months of everybody's time, the prospect narrowed it down to two vendors only. My company and our main competitor were both invited for a final demo to the entire selection committee, who openly disclosed the names of shortlisted vendors. Instead of going in with our standard assets, we decided to kill the competition and focus the entire demo on proving why we're better. My General Manager at that time literally downloaded the user manual of the product we were competing against and started looking for flaws or areas where we were doing a better job. After a much-focused Differentiation Demo, the project sponsor took us to his office where he had a binder with the scoring results for each of the 12 vendors evaluated and flipped our name with our competitors in the first position right in front of us.

Top 3 Takeaways:

The DIFFERENTIATION Demo	
#1	Requires intensive preparation and deep knowledge of your competitor' products and services. If in doubt, better to avoid any "demo bake-off."
#2	Is not meant to unprofessionally bash your competition. It officially gives the Demo Guru a chance to be more direct about the areas where the competition has inferior offerings.
#3	Should also include off-product items such as ability to execute, company viability, client base and customer satisfaction, etc.

The Scripted Demo

When organizations hire external consultants to help them with their software evaluation process, it is highly probable that the third party advisor compiled a demo script for all vendors to follow.

A Scripted Demo is a pre-defined list of demo items that have to be covered during the presentation, sometimes even following a specific order. The main purpose of this exercise is to provide a common way for the client to rate all vendors which, seen from the presales' standpoint, means that you will be scored and rated compared to your competitors. Sometimes, however, the list of items on the demo script and the sequence they appear in might not do justice to your product. It is crucial at this point to analyze the demo script and convert it from your worst enemy to your best friend, being respectful of the prospect's intentions.

The first thing to do when receiving a Scripted Demo is properly read each demo item and look for repeats; very often the same demo item appears in one section, only to be repeated in a later section. When that happens, try to understand why. Sometimes the prospect or the external advisor is using different verbiage that essentially means the same thing; maybe it is an actual repeat because the audiences will be different in the two sections, and both evaluating teams are interested in the same topic.

Secondly, while going through each demo item, it is necessary to map it to the exact functionality in the software that meets that requirement. Map them to a customer case study that will be presented or even simply mentioned during the demo. Minimally, each demo item should be mapped to a specific set of functionalities or demo assets that will prove that point in case you are asked, but the biggest value of this exercise is to identify real-life stories to be told while demoing specific items. Of course, this is also a good time for you to identify any area where the competition could perform better and plan accordingly.

Additionally, reorganize the proof points into a flow that best fits your product and allows you to tell a story while demoing. Make sure not to jump from one screen to another just to respect the order initially provided in the demo script, which could lead to your solution appearing complicated, disjointed, or unfriendly. It is good practice, in this case, to first ask the prospect or the external consultant running the evaluation if you are allowed to move the demo items around, reassuring them you will still cover all the proof points noted. Most of the time you will be able to swap things around, in which case during the demonstration it will be key to pause every once in a while and recap what you have shown, calling out the exact requirements you have covered in your session. This will allow your audience to go back to their scoring sheet and rate your performance.

Finally, keeping in mind that you *will* be scored, you do not want to leave the meeting without making sure you have responded to all of their questions and that there are no un-scored questions. Ask your audience if there are any proof points you have not covered yet and make sure you get a high score on those as well!

 **Recommendation:**

Always have an answer for each proof point on the demo script and reorganize the script into a logical flow to bring the highest value to your customer based on your solution. To make it easy for your audience to follow and to also gain credibility that you are indeed covering ALL of the points they wanted to score you on, prepare a simple leave behind. In the form of a Word table, add a column with their requirement ID and a description and a second column where you mention what session of the demo will cover that requirement with which functionality. Distribute this document to all attendees before beginning your presentation. This will make them feel safe you will cover their specific needs, paying more attention to what you are showing rather than their scoring sheet.

 Top 3 Takeaways:

The SCRIPTED Demo	
#1	Requires heavy preparation to map each required proof-point to the specific product functionality, demo asset, and customer story to be told.
#2	Might present demo proof-points that do not naturally fit with your preferred demo flow – in which case it is advisable to ask if the presentation order can be altered.
#3	Usually implies vendors will be rated, which requires the presenter to check in with the audience often to make sure they have all they need to perform their scoring.

The Rescue Demo

Not all demos go well. When they do not, the best Sales Engineer on the team is called for action! The Rescue Demo refers exactly to that—taking action and overhauling a situation.

These types of demos require a lot of strategic preparation and likely will be your last chance with that prospect. It's an uphill battle; you will have to play damage-control and fix what did not go well in the prior meetings. How do you do that? Talk to your team first, but, most importantly, talk to the prospect.

No matter how disillusioned your prospect is, the sales rep will have to get you on the phone with the project sponsor for you to understand from THEM what was not successful. Spruce up your listening skills. Make your prospect feel at ease, stating no one is trying to throw anybody under the bus, and have them be open with you. The only advantage of Rescue Demos is that the prospect will most likely be more open with you about what they liked and disliked about other solutions they have seen, thinking you will have zero chance at earning their business.

Now that we know what did not work in the past presentation right from the source, and we also know what impressed them from the competition, it is the sales rep's job to gain us a seat at the table AGAIN, and it is our job to start prepping. Focus on what you've been told to address and the relevant issues, and stay on track. Face the objections that were brought up since your last meeting before even venturing to demo anything else on your product and put those objections to sleep. Aim for feedback during your presentation.

Be sure to double down on your key differentiators and value statement only after successfully addressing and demystifying the initial concerns.

True Story: The Hail Mary Pass

I have been directly involved and heard about many situations when the feedback on the first demo to a prospect was not even slightly positive, but then, with a lot of preparation and a bit of luck, that same prospect became a customer. One of the most recent episodes was for a multi-million dollar deal in France. The local presales team did an outstanding job preparing an extremely comprehensive POC that, however, was perceived not to be "modern enough" by the evaluation team. Leveraging her phenomenal sales management skills, the GM of our France operation managed to have them debrief with us on what did not go well and most importantly persuaded them to give us another chance. The whole company from both sides of the ocean was now helping on that deal. Reaching out to our best resources, the local French team went back in and killed the demo. All the work we had all put in, preparing a response focused on showing how modern our solution could be, finally paid off, and we still now have the pleasure of serving that customer.

 Top 3 Takeaways:

The RESCUE Demo	
#1	Requires involving the most experienced Sales Engineer to reverse an unfavorable customer situation.
#2	Focuses on demystifying the initial concerns based on clear and honest guidance by the prospective customer agreeing to give our organization a second chance.
#3	Demands high empathy and human touch to deal with a disillusioned audience that has bad feelings about your solution.

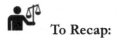

To Recap:

No matter what type of demo you embark on, there are some basic principles that apply to every circumstance. The grid below shows best practices that are applicable to any demonstration scenario and some typical mistakes of which to be mindful.

DEMO DELIVERY	
What to Do	**What Not to Do**
Tailor your demo to your audience	Focus on features and functions
Map "proof points" to the agenda	Stick to the demo flow
Differentiate	Get lost in the weeds
Engage your audience	Wait until the end for the WOW effect
Prove your worth	Be afraid to park questions
Involve Customer Success	Speak for the entire meeting
Show eagerness and passion	Underestimate demo equipment
Coordinate with your sales counterpart	

Extra Tip!

Add a quiz. As much as we do not like long presentations, sometimes the customer selection process involves meeting with many vendors for several hours in a short amount of time. We will talk more in the following pages on how to leverage and surf the attention curve when in front of an audience, but one technique that was proposed to me by a prospective customer was to add a quiz during the demo. When calling for a break, or maybe after an intensive session, it might be a good idea to spruce it up with a quick Product Quiz. Simply throw up a pre-arranged slide with some trivial questions about the functionality you have just presented and have your audience compete for the right answer!

We will wrap up this chapter on "Demo Types" by presenting two additional types of demonstration that Demo Gurus often find themselves dealing with: the annoying "POC" and the dreaded "Workshop."

Proof of Concept

I have lost track of the number of times I heard my salesforce suggesting a proof of concept, or POC, to their prospective customers. Proofs of concept are extremely intensive and require a lot of work and attention. They should not merely replicate the As-Is situation of a prospect demanding a proof of concept; they should instead show how your solution can meet the requirement or concept the prospect wants to be proven and extend to other areas that could bring additional value to your customer's future situation.

Proofs of concept can be your best weapon or lead a path to failure if not properly staffed, analyzed, implemented, and delivered.

To successfully deliver a Proof of Concept:

- Make sure it is happening at the right stage of an active sales cycle. There is no reason why the first touchpoint with a prospect would be a fully custom POC. Try to understand the evaluation process of your prospect, look for an RFP, or simply talk to your project sponsors to understand what happens next. As a rule of thumb, you should be embarking on a proof of concept only when you know your product has been shortlisted as a finalist.

- Make sure you are playing a fair game. Customers should require all shortlisted vendors to go through the same exercise within a common timeframe and should try to support them indistinctively in the most unbiased way. Of course, any software company with confidence in its solution would prefer to be chosen as the only vendor having to conduct a POC; however, usually a head-to-head bake-off is the second-best choice. The goal in this case is to make sure you are not putting any hours into something that politically or strategically you know will not have a fair chance of translating into an actual sale.

- Demand free access and participation from your customer's evaluation team. As with any touchpoint during the sales cycle, it is fundamental to access your audience and start building rapport with them way before the day of the official presentation. Ask your salesperson to organize clarification calls after you have analyzed the data provided and look for errors—it's a great opportunity to ask intelligent questions and start building your credibility. Not having access to the right people from your customer's side as much as needed is a red flag that could derail the whole sale cycle.

- Clearly define the scope of the POC and the goals your prospect intends to achieve. While reviewing the exact topics that will be included in the proof of concept, stay away from trivial proof points that will not be bringing any value to the customer and that will just waste your time. Basic proof items, such as "make sure you can turn on your computer" or other points that could be easily proven by the fact that you have hundreds of customers doing exactly that, should not have the dignity to be part of a POC. Reject those and focus the attention more on the points that represent a competitive advantage for your solution and clearly define the Success Criteria the prospect is looking to address to define a POC successful.

These few considerations show how labor-intensive POCs are and the level of expense and effort they potentially represent for an organization.

Depending on the complexity of the use case to prove, you could have one or more members of your team out of pocket building the POC for multiple days. You might even request help from other departments in the organization to come up with the most appropriate positioning and value for your prospect, which substantially adds more costs to the sales cycle.

For this reason, it is fundamental that your prospect gets some "skin in the game": demand they share with you their next steps, openly stating that a purchase of your solution should follow if all the agreed-upon success factors will be met.

If they are not willing to agree on that, think about this opportunity twice!

PROOF OF CONCEPT	
What to Do	**What Not to Do**
Understand the buying cycle	Immediately jump to POCs to start with
Clearly define scope and success factors	Simply replicate the AS-IS situation
Demand access to the evaluation team	Use customer's data for the most basic proof points
Demand a competitive but fair process	
Demand customer's "skin in the game"	

True Story: Totally Missed the Mark

This is a very peculiar sales cycle I experienced recently. After two full years of engagement, the prospective customer from a government software company asked us to deliver a Proof of Concept based on specific use cases. The audience was so committed to making it happen that they even agreed to pay us a fee, knowing the considerable amount of time and resources that this POC would require. They also sent us specific use cases that had to be replicated with exact steps, almost down to the individual clicks. The POC team was happy because what was required was nothing too crazy and was something that the software team could easily handle. We involved the prospect throughout the build, picked their brains, and asked for guidance. In a few days, we were done and ready to present the POC back to the entire team. The result? This client decided not to go ahead with the purchase. Why? The POC did not show that much differentiation from what they already had in place. We simply replicated their AS-IS process and lost the deal.

 Recommendation:

Less-educated prospects sometimes tend to add items in their checklist that are basic must-haves that any of the vendors they are reaching out to will be able to meet. While this might seem like a "quick win" for the vendors (demonstrating something that their products can handle without a glitch), in reality, they bring no value to the prospect and more importantly, do not allow you to differentiate. It's like shopping for a CRM solution comparing Salesforce.com with Microsoft Dynamics CRM and asking the two organizations to show they can send email notifications when a lead is assigned to a salesperson. They would not be in business if they could not do that. The point here is this: try to focus on the value of the requirement that needs to be demonstrated and explain this to your audience during your preparation calls, especially when dealing with first-timers to product evaluations.

Workshop

Customer workshops are some of the most intensive and stressful activities a Sales Engineer will go through. Workshops represent focused study groups where prospective customers require vendors to build a solution tailored to their needs, right in front of them, with the ultimate goal of experiencing how the solution comes to life and how to use it first-hand.

Sometimes these types of events are simply about allowing the prospective customer to "play" with your solution; other times, they assume the format of a mini-project over several days, if not months.

No matter the format and the related level of effort required by the workshop, similar considerations that were discussed in the previous section for POCs apply to workshops, as well. Make sure these activities happen at the right stage of the sales cycle; understand who else from the competition has been asked to do the same, and demand a clear action from the prospective customer in case the workshop is successful.

One-day workshops aiming to solely have your prospective customers get their hands on your solution are becoming more and more frequent in the world of software sales.

Prospects are becoming more skeptical about shiny demos that impeccable sales engineers have now mastered to perfection, and they want to experience your solution directly. When this happens, make sure you are adequately prepared so that your hands-on workshops run as smoothly as possible:

- Leverage a dedicated infrastructure to help with your workshop. This should include a set of pre-defined use cases you want your prospective customers to go through, together with adequate training materials and videos with step-by-step instructions. The goal of this detailed documentation is to prevent your prospect from getting lost in your solution and starting to poke around without understanding what needs to be done.

- Regardless of what use case you want your attendees to go through, first present it yourself to the full audience; go to the podium and use a projector to walk them through the use case they will be doing by themselves. For the most complicated use cases, break them in chunks, and have your prospects follow you along as you click through the case study.

- If it is a multi-user workshop, have someone from your team walk through the desks to make sure every attendee is following your instructions and no one is left behind. This will help get everybody to stay on track in case anyone "missed a click" while you are presenting.

- Limit the user interaction only to those areas of the software that are of interest to the workshop. The more menu items available to your users, the more they will try to randomly click to explore things on their own.

Multiple-day workshops are instead more challenging as they involve all the considerations, effort, and attention of a production project but in a more condensed timeline and hopefully on a limited scale. In this case:

- Schedule adequate pre-meeting calls with your prospects to understand exactly what they want to achieve with the workshop and what its success factors are. Ask for detailed proof points; simply stating they want to get more comfortable with the "look and feel" of your solution will not justify a full-blown out workshop.

- Staff your workshops with the right blend of solution experts and subject matter experts. During these meetings, your prospects will probably explain what their requirements are for the first time; you need to have someone that understands and is experienced with the topics they want to cover. Having someone from the Professional Services organization that can explain how other customers have addressed the same requirement could be very useful.

- Demand a restricted team from the customer's side. Having the entire Finance, Marketing, or Sales teams participate in a workshop is counterproductive, probably resulting in personalized interests, requests, or side discussions that will derail the initial intent. Make sure instead to interact only with a core team representing the interests of the entire team, and finish up your workshop with a presentation to the executive team illustrating the scope of the workshop, providing feedback on how it was run and reflecting on whether or not it met the expectations. Remember to thank your prospect's core team in front of the larger executive audience!

- Say you need time. The pressure these events could put on you is sometimes enormous. Right when you think you have the situation under control, the prospect asks you why that number does not tie to their excel-run models after comparing your results to their own. You know your number is right, but you need to understand what your solution is doing; do not be afraid to ask for some time. Ask for a break, so you do not have five pairs of eyes on you, and focus on your issue; all you have to do here is manage your anxiety and stay focused.

WORKSHOP	
What to Do	**What Not to Do**
Understand the scope	Agree to everything you are being asked
Bring a subject matter expert	Be afraid to ask for more time
Work with a limited Core Team	
Remember you are still selling	
Stress and pressure management	

True Story: My Name on the Contract!

People make the difference. This story is probably one of my most challenging experiences as a Sales Engineer, made easier, however, thanks to a great customer relationship we were able to build over the course of a five-day workshop. My senior consultant and I went to Quebec for an important onsite workshop; we knew very little about how the prospect operated and how detailed they wanted to be with this initiative. It turned out their requirements were outrageously complicated and not even close to what we thought they would be. Once we realized the situation, we did all the right things: we asked the prospect not to have all the end users in the room with us eight hours a day but only a couple of them. We spent hours discussing their requirements and even more hours thinking about a possible solution back at the hotel. We proved our worth by talking their language and challenging their requests just after a couple of days together in their business. And yes, both my senior consultant's name and mine were part of the contract!

 **Recommendation:**

Always double-check the logistics of your meeting and make sure your technical equipment will allow for a smooth experience. Always bring your projector, travel with some universal adaptors, and bring your hot-spot if you need internet access. Demo logistics and equipment could easily account for a full chapter of this book, but I will leave it up to you to use your best judgment to make sure you have all the technology in place to deliver a trouble-free demo! With your technical checklist crossed off, keep in mind those soft skills any sales engineer should leverage in any type of demo. Refer to the upcoming chapters to learn more about connecting with your audience, effectively answering questions, and complementing your product demo with proper non-verbal communication.

Chapter 2.4 – Phase 3: Post Demo Musts

At this point, you have performed a phenomenal presentation; all the attendees were following along and asking intelligent questions, commenting on how your solution can help them in many areas, and some of them even came to shake your hand and commend you on your demonstration. But guess what? You are not done until the contract is signed!

Too often, the Sales Engineer is taken off the shelf, dusted off, thrust in front of the client to demo and answer technical questions, and then is retired back to the shelf until the next demo.

Yes, the tension and pressure of your live demo are now off, but you and your salesperson still have very important tasks to work on together.

In the following few pages, we will highlight some key steps to plan for after a successful demo.

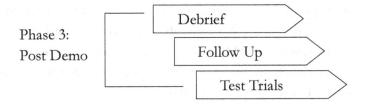

Figure 2.4.1. Main steps of the Post Demo Phase of the Sales Cycle

Internal Debrief

Make sure you spend adequate time considering what went wrong, what was successful, or what could have simply gone better after your demonstration. A simple "I think it went well, let's see what they say" while stepping out of your customer's office will not do the job. You and your salesperson need to formally jump on a debrief call to understand how the meeting went. Share your read on the room, who the most engaged attendees were, what resonated with them, any non-disclosed info on the competition you were able to grasp, any additional opportunity you can identify, or any outstanding items that require immediate follow-up. Discuss any partner involvement that could help you seal the deal or evaluate the idea of having your CEO write a Thank You email to your prospect's management team. Simply put, BE PROACTIVE, and discuss WHAT'S NEXT.

A debrief meeting is not a fighting arena where everybody complains. There is no finger-pointing at anybody, especially if the meeting did not live up to the expectations. It is rather a critical moment for you and your salesperson to learn how to work better together and most importantly to brainstorm on additional value selling for your prospect.

Debriefs should not just be internal, however.

As already alluded to, the biggest mistake after a flawless demonstration is to think that the team nailed it and the presentation was unconditionally superb. To confirm your feelings and validate your assumptions, you must fact-check your hypothesis with the prospective customer. If you and your salesperson have established a trusted relationship with your customer, you should be able to gain unbiased feedback on your performance directly from your project sponsor, if not the same day, then the day following your presentation.

As a preference, I try not to be on the line for the very first debrief with the customer and instead let my account executive run those directly with the prospect to have them be as open as possible.

This entire debrief process is worthless if no action is taken. The result of a debriefing session is a clear list of To-Dos with related priorities. You need to be proactive and help your account executive move the deal forward by collaborating with your future client.

DEBRIEF	
What to Do	**What Not to Do**
Critically assess the situation	Think you are done with the demo
Provide open feedback to your team	Provoke or initiate finger-pointing
Strive for feedback from customer	Think the demo was great without client validation
List out To Dos and priorities	
Be proactive and take action	

 **Recommendation:**

We are all exhausted but hopefully satisfied after a long demonstration. The idea of having to do more for that prospect gives us the chills, but it's fundamental we do not give up. I am fully convinced that way less than 50% of the sale occurs during the demo itself. A good 40% happens before the demo through relationship building and education, and a healthy 30% happens after the demo through constant follow-up, differentiation, and value selling. Understanding how to use that 30% is vital to the success of any sale. Do not accept any call from your sales team asking for an additional "in-depth demo" if you do not even know how the first one was received;

demand feedback and action items right after the presentation. Do not let too many days go by since it will make recollection harder; make it a point for your sales force interaction to schedule demo debriefs and action plans after each presentation.

Follow-up

You now know what to do. You have discussed and confirmed your priorities with your account executive, and it is now time to translate plans into actions and actions into results.

The paradigm for any action you take from this moment forward is the quality and timeliness of your follow-ups. You do not want to provide any information that is not specifically relevant to what your prospect asked for, jeopardizing all the good work you've done so far (yes, don't screw it up now!). Provide all applicable information in a timely fashion, and keep your word, especially if you have committed or even simply mentioned a timely follow up to any question you had to park during the demonstration. If someone else is holding you up and you are not able to provide feedback within the timeframe you have "committed" to, quickly draft a note to your project sponsors and notify them you are still working on their questions. Letting them know you have not forgotten about them makes them feel well taken care of, and it's an easy, two-minute email on your side.

Follow-ups will vary depending on the specific questions asked during your presentation. In general, however, we see the following as good practices, some of these going beyond the obvious review of those items that are now clearly sitting on your plate as a result of the presentation:

- Help craft a personalized Value Statement email your account executive will send to the evaluation team. I hate generic Thank You emails (except those your CEO will write!) that are sent out just "to be nice." Any touchpoint that brings no value to your customer is simply an annoying sales endeavor your prospect will pick up on. Your customer has probably gone through an excruciating selection process, evaluating many vendors that all look alike and say the same thing. Use this touchpoint as a way to re-state what they have seen in YOUR presentation, focus on those items that resulted in a WOW effect during your live presentation, and remind them why your company and solution will bring the most VALUE to them.

- At a minimum, follow up on any outstanding item. We will see in the pages to come how it is totally fine to say, "I do not know the answer to this, and I will get back to you" during a demonstration. The key here is to live up to your promise. Diligently research the question you were not able to, or did not want to, answer live during the presentation and come up with a clear and effective write up you can send your prospect. The write up could be in the form of a quick email if the question to follow up on allows it or, even better, a leave-behind that describes step by step how that topic is addressed in your solution. Be concise and to the point with your leave-behind and include screenshots to support your explanation; this will avoid a potential request from your prospect to see more.

- Send relevant content. Many topics usually come up during a demo that have nothing to do with the product. Or maybe you did not have time to cover several topics for one reason or another. Digital assets are probably the best and most effective follow up technique to educate your prospect on your company, solution, and the value you will bring to them. Direct your project sponsors to case studies covering similar needs or challenges that came up during the live demo with clear examples of how some of your existing customers have already faced and resolved the same issues with your solution. Propose live events like roadshows or seminars your marketing team is planning in the short term as an opportunity for your prospects to meet with your customers and hear their experience with your solution first hand. Send over market research and trends to show them how your company and product are in line with the latest market direction, or simply tap into those marketing collaterals to follow up on additional uses of your solution that could be helpful to your customer's long-term vision.

- Offer a free study group with your Subject Matter Experts. Depending on the level of complexity of your solution and the financial and/or strategic value of the opportunity you are working on, an effective way to keep your solution at the top of your customer's mind is to offer a free consultation. During this time, your customer success team will spend some time with the customer's evaluation team to discuss their needs. We are not proposing an additional product demonstration; we are suggesting a consultative session where prospects can discuss their requirements in detail and, most importantly, get to experience a key component of your product and company DNA that is often not adequately represented in the sales cycle: your customer success team.

FOLLOW-UP	
What to Do	**What Not to Do**
Send resolution on any outstanding item	Think you are done with the demo
Craft a value-selling follow up email	Miss shared follow-up dates
Send additional relevant content	Propose another demo as a follow-up
Offer free study groups with SMEs	
Be proactive and take action	

Test Trial

Together with workshops and hands-on POCs, test trials respond to your prospect's willingness to try your solution first-hand, usually in an independent way, without you or your team looking after them.

The goal of a test trial, which is also usually offered free of charge to your prospects as part of the sales cycle, is to confirm how easy your solution is. It is rarely to verify if your solution is indeed capable of delivering on what you promised during the demonstration. In the world of enterprise software sales, no matter how intuitive your solution or product is, I hardly believe that any of your prospective users will be able to start using your products like a professional, translating their requirements into effective implementations without any sort of training first. A test trial is an opportunity for the prospect to experience working with the solution, not to replicate their exact requirements in a short amount of time.

Make sure your salesperson sets the right expectation when proposing a test trial, which leads us to the main question: When should a test trial be offered?

Test trials ARE NOT sales tools. Test trials are instead a CLOSING tool and, as such, they should be used and offered wisely. Test trials do not help your sales velocity and potential success because of two reasons.

First, they naturally lengthen the sales cycle with an additional touchpoint: it would be any sales engineer's dream to contribute to a sale without showing any features or functions and a salespersons' dream to close a deal in the shortest amount of time. Test trials typically extend over several weeks and sometimes months. During this time, you have no control over your prospect, and besides annoying "How is it going?" emails or checking the activity logs, there is very little you can do. Not only are they in the driver's seat with you right next to them in the passenger seat, but they also decide how fast to drive or when to stop.

Secondly, test trials introduce a level of risk you do not want to add to your sales cycle. As confident as you might be about your product offering and as easy to use, flexible, or intuitive it might be, remember you are still selling to an untrained crowd whose instinct will be that of clicking or touching anywhere, trying to break your product without you watching.

These few items should make your salespeople aware of the potential downsides a free trial could have on their sales cycle. However, test trials can be very powerful weapons when used as a closing technique instead of a sales tool.

You should not rely on a generic, all-encompassing, or unfocused event to sell your product, but you can leverage it when you have gone through a tailored sales process and now need some extra help to close your deal. Offering a product trial when you know you are head-to-head with a competitor that does not offer any trials of its solution could be a great closing strategy. Use your product trial at the right stage of the sales cycle to differentiate from the competition and to demonstrate to your prospect the confidence you have in your solution.

When a free trial is the way to go, it is critical to follow a few best practices to maximize its closing potential and limit its inherent risks:

- Duration: Research proves that most of the time, free trials in software evaluations are mostly for the customer's "ease of mind" to make sure the vendors are not lying about what they have been promoting in their past presentations, especially when it comes to the highly-inflated "ease of use" every vendor oversells. Trial users usually log in the moment they have been granted access from a spike of motivation and curiosity, poke around for a few minutes, click around without a clear purpose in mind, and more times than not, it is the only exposure they will have with your trial. Very few times, you are lucky enough to find users that follow your recommendations and read your online step-by-step tutorials. Exactly for this reason, trials should be limited in time; many SaaS solutions offer 30-day trials, which is a long time for your salesperson to be in the passenger's seat. My suggestion is to give less time to your prospects to test your solution (a week or ten days in the more sophisticated software industry is the standard), forcing them to factually connect to your solution and allowing your salesperson to engage back with them sooner (keeping your cost of sales down in the meantime).

- Infrastructure: Your trial solution needs to scream ease of use for your trial users to have an enjoyable experience checking out your solution. Make sure no add-ons have to be installed on any machine to make the trial experience as plug-and-play as possible. Limit access to your overall features and functions; leverage a restricted license of your solution that only encompasses a selection of your most frequently used functionalities, which also most adequately sets you apart from the competition. Complement your trial use cases with comprehensive documentation for online tutorials and, most importantly, through quick, digital How-To videos that are easy to consult for your trial users. If possible, leverage an auditing and tracking mechanism with on-demand chat support. This way you will be notified of any error your trial user received while exploring the solution, and your support team will be able to proactively contact your prospect and offer an explanation to his or her error.

- Offer an introductory trial walk-through. To make it easy for your trial users, set up a quick web meeting to guide your users through the trial infrastructure; show them how to use its many assets, such as videos or tutorials, and make sure everybody can connect without any problem. In the case of extended trials, also offer up multiple touch-points to get the testing team together and assess progress.

As part of your follow-up strategy with your salesperson, you should accurately contemplate the benefits of employing a free trial in your sales cycle.

Evaluate the alternatives to free trials, keeping in mind there are other ways to have your prospects experience your solution. Workshops and hands-on POCs have already been discussed, however, let your salesperson be creative from a negotiation perspective, considering the potential for no-obligation contracts or money-back guarantees.

These are powerful closing techniques your sales force could be adopting to instill the same sense of reassurance your prospect is looking for with a test trial but with less risk.

True Story: Nosy Customers!

Giving software away for testing purposes is like giving a new toy to a three-year-old boy: he looks at it, tries to break it, and forgets about it after two days. After five days, you'll ask him if he liked his new toy, and he'll say he did. The same experience occurs with multi-year professionals that want to test drive your solution. When we first released our free-trial package at my current company, we were so proud of it and could not wait for people to start using it. We had worked months to make it perfect and, I must say, we got pretty close to perfection! After just a few weeks of being live with our first release, we finally got asked for a free trial. To the exact opposite of everything I discussed above, we immediately agreed. We went full steam ahead with the trial set up, sent log-in instructions, and even walked the users through a quick live preview of the trial functionality. Then, we let our prospect go with it. Every half an hour, we checked in to see what they were doing. Disappointingly enough, through our auditing capabilities, we saw they were just looking at a video here or reading a tutorial there, and we realized that the most visited page on the whole trial infrastructure was our picture page. Every user kept going back to that page where we had pictures of the team members working that opportunity—our GM, Account Executive, etc. They were all more interested in learning about us than our product. People buy from people!

TEST TRIALS	
What to Do	**What Not to Do**
Use them as a closing tool	Promote them as part of any sales strategy
Closely monitor prospect's activity	Agree to prolonged access
Rely on adequate trial infrastructure	Send log-ins without any prior walkthrough
Schedule a trial walk-through	
Evaluate alternatives to trial applications	

Chapter 2.5 – Connecting with Your Audience

Charisma and empathy are two must-haves of any presenter. The ability to connect with your audience by gaining their interest, keeping them engaged, and giving them the feeling you are not just lecturing them, but that you instead understand their most common daily struggles, is particularly important for any Sales Engineer's success.

Connecting to your audience is not an easy task. Usually, that connection kicks in when you feel the energy flow between you and your listeners—when you realize your audience is flattered by what you are saying and are giving them a memorable experience.

To use an expression from Osborn, it is all about "immediacy," which reflects the "desire to communicate a closeness between speakers and listeners." In other words, immediacy is used to reduce the distance between the speaker and the audience. The utmost revelation of immediacy is that of a likable presenter talking to an engaged audience.

True Story: My First Sales Kick-Off Presentation

I am a people's person; I enjoy company, hate working remotely, and I am naturally inclined to make people feel at ease. All of this, coupled with many years of research and practice, definitely helps a lot with my job as a presenter. It was the very first sales kick-off meeting I ever attended. I had never done an official demonstration before, and it was the last session of the day before the cocktail hour. The room was packed with partners, resellers, and internal employees. As soon as I got in, I could tell from everybody's face they had no interest in listening to a 20-something-year-old kid who just got out of college. However, just like instructed, I began my presentation, and I proudly overwhelmed my audience with statistics and facts to demonstrate how good I was despite my young age. Luckily enough, five minutes into the presentation, I bumped into one of the attendees shaking his head, almost in full desperation mode. Defying all my plans and hard preparation, I moved away from my podium and started talking about their current situation, how bored they all were, and how they couldn't wait to go get the cocktail hour in the adjacent room. I told them I could fix that. Instead of having me go through my endless deck for the next 45 minutes, I invited the audience to ask me directly what they needed, obviously related to the topic of the session I was presenting. For every solution I had, they had to listen to one of my stats. We kept going well beyond the 45 minutes and could even hear people cheering and toasting in the nearby room, but we were too focused on "our own stuff." Without knowing, I had just made it about them and not me, in a very personal, likable manner.

Connecting with your audience starts from the time you shake hands (or simply bow a la Japanese in the era of global pandemics) at the beginning of your meeting, or the instant you introduce yourself on a webcast, to the moment you leave the room or disconnect your web session.

During this time, you have to constantly jump into your customers' world, one step at a time, having them perceive you as "one of them," and having them see you as a colleague they would like to have on their team.

Probably one of the clearest and most obvious signs that you have boosted your immediacy with your audience is when they openly ask for you to personally attend any further meetings or, even more rewarding, when they want to condition signing a contract only if your name appears on it as one of the stakeholders of their initiative.

Talking to your audience is usually perceived as two-way communication between two main actors: the speaker and the listener. I like to think, instead, that there is a third component in any communication that even if not physically present plays a key role in the communication: your topic of discussion.

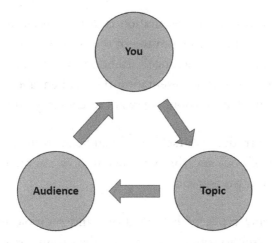

Figure 2.5.1. The Circle of Communication

To be effective, you need to connect first yourself with the topic you are talking about, then connect to your audience, which in turn will find your content intriguing and of interest. If you are dropping any of these three elements, your conversation will be just a sterile talk. Connecting with your audience requires constantly orchestrating these three elements to guarantee a memorable experience for your listeners.

General Considerations

No matter what type of audience you are dealing with, some basic behaviors always apply. In the next few pages, we will be covering some key aspects that affect connecting with your audience that any presenter should keep at the top of his or her mind:

- Perfecting your introduction

- Making it personal

- Remembering the "attention curve"

Perfect Your Intro

Learning how to start a presentation is just as important as knowing how to finish it. It is the beginning of the conversation that can make or break capturing your audience's attention. We often forget that there are many ways to start a presentation that will engage the hearts and minds of the people to whom you want to convey your message.

The way you introduce yourself to your audience is the first impression they will get of you, and that will dictate how attentive they will be throughout your presentation.

There are many types of introductions and multiple techniques to introduce yourself to your audience, typically varying based on the type of event you are attending and the geography you are in.

This chapter is not intended to describe how you should present yourself in situations that sales engineers usually are not involved with, such as kicking off a Conference or giving a TED Talk (maybe some of us do give TED Talks, but not all of us!) Rather, it focuses on how you should word your introduction to grasp your audience's attention during a typical client meeting or a product demonstration, as part of a bigger sales or marketing event.

Let's take a look at these two types of introductions.

Introduction One:

"Hi everyone, my name is Alessio Lolli, and I am the Vice President of Product Experience for XYZ Incorporated, and I work directly for Mark, here, on my left. I have been with the company for three years now, but I have spent almost 15 years selling software to the Top 500 organizations. I have worked with more than 100 customers within XYZ Inc., and I hope you can join the family soon."

Introduction Two:

"Hi everyone, my name is Alessio Lolli, and I am in charge of what we call Product Experience at XYZ. What that means is that I represent the liaison between the market needs that I explore through customers' presentations, workshops, or any other activity in the fields and our development center to make sure our software responds to our customers' needs. Today, I will be walking you through how our solution can help you with your Sales Pipeline Reporting needs."

Both introductions are admittedly relatively quick; it takes probably less than a minute to go through them individually, and your audience usually appreciates quick introductions as they are eager to get to the demo and see your solution in action.

There are, however, noticeable differences between the two types of introductions that could be summarized with the following best practices:

- Avoid stating your title. Generally, in the past few years, we have let our imagination prevail when it comes to job positions. From product evangelists and company ambassadors to architects and even sales engineers, some people interpret all these titles as a bit high-sounding and it might make no sense to them. Some other attendees might be intimated by the title you have and even feel scared or embarrassed by your "Global Vice President of Operations" title. As proud as you might be of your high-ranked position, there are many other ways to phrase that you are responsible for a specific area in your organization. Introduction Two is a good example in that respect. Instead of stating a corporate title that implies power and responsibility, it gets the same concept and message across but in a more modest and less "formal" way. Similarly, stay away from lengthy dissertations of your past jobs, accomplishments, and successes; you could come across as bragging for achievements from 5-10 years before that may not be even applicable anymore in today's world. The first type of introduction conveys exactly that idea; it is all centered on how great and successful your career has been over the past few years and could come across as arrogant. It may be more suited for a job interview than a sales call where all you want to do is to establish yourself as a subject matter expert.

- Clearly state the value you bring to your organization. If you work for an organization, the assumption is that you bring some kind of value to your company; that is something you should be proud of and should share with your audience. Explain what your role is within the organization and how you contribute to its success without going into useless excruciating details. Make your audience understand why you are an important asset to your organization. The second type of introduction does a very good job explaining the role of a sales engineer beyond pure demos. It focuses on how sales engineers—being always in the field, in touch with many different organizations, and constantly hit by the competition—factually help their companies and products advance, improve, and deliver better value for their customers. Shifting the focus from what you do to the value you bring to your organization will make your audience more interested in what you have to tell them and will reinforce your image of a trusted advisor for them.

- Clearly state what you will be doing during the meeting. Once you have explained how you contribute to your company's success, openly and quickly state what your role in the meeting will be, as people like to understand what everybody will contribute. Prospective customers, in particular, are very aware of their advantageous position as buyers and love to hear how you will be helping them. Again, Introduction Two is a good example of how to explain to your audience what you will be doing for them during the meeting. Not simply a demo, but a tailored presentation aiming to show them how you and your solution will address their current situation and the value it will bring to them, hitting some of the key requirements you have learned of from your past discoveries.

Overall, even in introductions where you usually would think it is about you, it is in reality about how you will be helping your customers and what they will be getting by attentively listening to you. Make it about them and not about you right from the start; this will set the bar for the course of the entire presentation as your prospect will be already intrigued by what you are going to show them to make their lives easier.

Finally, as with everything else, practice your introduction to perfection. Especially with repetitive tasks like introductions, refining your intro off-stage is essential to make sure you start your presentation on the right foot!

 **Recommendation:**

Quite often, sales engineers are also requested to perform product demonstrations in front of large audiences that involve hundreds of users. Examples of these types of events could be industry conferences, user group conferences, or product launch webinars, where the considerations illustrated above could not be wholly applicable. In fact, in case of large audience presentations where sales engineers have to provide a quick product demonstration maybe even as part of the keynote speech, the recommendation is to start by making an impact right away. You will probably have already been introduced through a general announcement or directly by the colleague that calls you on stage, therefore there is no need to restate your role and position. Instead, it is all about starting "big." Truth be told, I am not a fan of long, rehearsed jokes, which to me sound just like that—rehearsed; but I am all in favor of any strategy that could almost shock or intrigue the audience. And that sometimes can happen through non-verbal skills: your pace, the tone of your voice, and the enthusiasm you show as soon as you step on the stage and start your demonstration are way more powerful tools than any line you might have rehearsed.

 Top 3 Takeaways:

During Your Introduction...	
#1	Avoid stating your title or exposing your resume.
#2	Focus on the value you bring to your own organization to explain your roles and responsibilities.
#3	Clearly state your role for the meeting at hand and how you will help your audience during the presentation.

Make It Personal

We are all humans—even the crankiest executives or the most closeted purchasing officers all have emotions! Together, with your sales counterpart, it is your responsibility as a likable sales engineer to build a human relationship with your prospective customer's evaluation team, hoping to get any of its members to become your future "sponsor." A study conducted by the International Data Corporation (IDC) concluded that all things being equal, buyers are more inclined to buy from people they feel they can have a mutual relationship of support and trust. Building that relationship requires showing empathy with your prospects—both with what is directly related to their current work routines but also with anything unrelated to their daily job—to capitalize on that human factor that all relationships thrive on.

A personal touch will naturally lead your audience to perceive you and your company as less of a solution provider and as more of a trusted advisor that puts them and their needs at the center of attention. To do this:

- Focus on them: Use the product as a launching pad to focus on their issues and how you will fix them. Instead of rushing to the screen to show how powerful your solution is, introduce each functionality you want to demo by first explaining a common issue they have probably experienced. On one side, this will allow you to gauge the level of interest your audience has in what you are about to show, but most importantly it shows that you are familiar with their common pains and struggles. Take a moment to challenge their current practices and show genuine curiosity about their current processes and the rationale behind them; all of it without touching your solution or product. Give your audience what they want and get rid of what they do not want to make it relevant to them. Speaking their language and focusing on their needs rather than commending how great your product is or how better you are than the competition will naturally attract your buyers and will increase their trust in you, which is the ultimate reason why people buy from people.

- Tell a story: Prospective customers are always very curious to learn what their peers are doing. This especially holds true with C-level executives who take pride in proving what they are already doing or plan on doing is in line with their peers facing the same struggles. The goal of storytelling is not to lecture your audience, neither is it to make them feel they are missing the mark. It is rather to show them they are not alone with their issues—that their peers, too, are struggling in a very similar fashion but have been able to improve their situations by embracing your products and solutions. The first step to successful storytelling is to find a good story to tell; go back to your discovery notes and pick out those items that represent the toughest challenges for your prospect and see how other customers of yours have fixed similar situations. Storytelling is an extraordinary example of human-to-human connection rather than human-to-product. It is also an extremely powerful tool, especially when the story can be backed up with quantitative and measurable statistics of how your other customers have benefitted from your solution.

- Honor their work and company: People like to be told they did a good job! Elevator rides are the best occasions for you to commend the work your sponsor has done so far, assisting you and your team in preparing for your meeting. Especially when an intense RFP process is issued, make sure to acknowledge the (hopefully) good quality of the questions asked. People who are also proud employees of their companies like to talk about their organization; use that walk to the conference room to ask questions about how the staff is organized on the floor and show interest and curiosity in always-present awards and product samples that are usually showcased in the waiting area.

True Story: The Italian Connection

My Italian background has often helped me connect with my audience in any geography, especially when people with Italian descent were in the room! Many years ago, I got a call from one of my salespeople saying they absolutely needed me on a demo. Quite flattered, I felt important and proud of myself; the top sales rep in my organization wanted me to help him with his deal. We got on the phone and the sales rep told me the main decision maker is a passionate gentleman with an Italian background that sounded very proud of his heritage. Fairly disappointed that he did not call me for my good qualities as a sales engineer, I still showed up at the customer's office on the day of my presentation. As soon as I introduced myself and pronounced my name, it was like being back in Rome, enjoying some pasta and vino with my best friend. He was a hardcore Italian immigrant from the 80s, extremely nostalgic of his birthplace, and we spent a good 20 minutes talking about Italy and what we missed the most. The references to the "bel paese" kept coming up during the demo, and I could tell in my new best friend's eyes he was proud of me! In all honesty, I do not think I delivered a perfect demo that day, but that Italy talk won us the deal! People buy from people.

Top 3 Takeaways:

To Make it Personal...	
#1	Make it about them. Show interest in your customer's current processes, needs, and politely challenge their status quo.
#2	Leverage storytelling to show your customers how their peers had the same challenges and how they were able to overcome them with your solution.
#3	Show empathy by referring to your audience by name, commending their hard work, or commenting on a recent public company announcement.

Remember the Attention Curve

Any conference attendee or meeting participant is supposedly willing to listen and pay attention to you; however, those same listeners are also easily distracted.

There are several reasons why your audience might get distracted.

Maybe you are the last presenter of a three-day evaluation marathon, and your audience is physically tired of listening to similar topics and "selly" pitches. Or, maybe an emergency has come up, and your listeners are multi-tasking, keeping an ear on what you are saying and an eye on their emails. Or your presentation is simply not interesting enough for them.

From the inadequate and sometimes even unreadable slide deck you are using to the passive tone of your voice, you are simply giving them no reason to listen to you.

Grabbing the attention of your audience and, most importantly, retaining it throughout the presentation is not an easy task in today's world.

Expressions like "Attention Scarcity" or "Attention Economy" have become increasingly popular in the past few years. Attention is identified as a resource and, as such, is by definition limited and potentially scarce. In the information-rich world we live in, we are struggling to gain attention from whom we want to talk; ask your marketing department what they were doing ten years ago to increase traffic. The answer is probably publishing more content. Fast forward to today's era and we now are experiencing an overload of information that our minds are not able to process adequately.

As the pioneer of attention economics Herbert A. Simon says, the "wealth of information creates a poverty of attention, and a need to allocate that attention efficiently among the overabundance of information sources that might consume it."

When giving a presentation, as Sales Engineers, we must realize that we will not be able to keep our audience's sole attention for the entire duration of our presentation. It helps, however, to understand what messages to deliver and what key points to make if we are aware of the typical attention span attendees usually have during a presentation and how to maximize that period of exclusive focus.

Let's start by analyzing first how the average audience pays attention during a typical presentation of 45 to 60 minutes in length. Gibbs' 1992 Attention Curve illustration is still very timely:

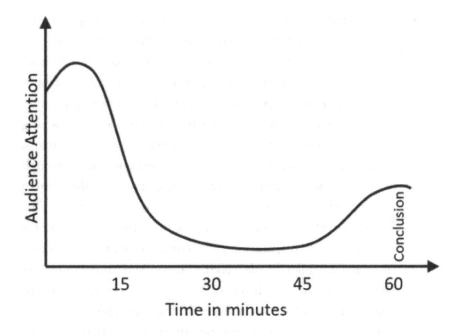

Figure 2.5.2. Typical Attention Curve

The chart above shows that:

- Almost everyone is extremely focused at the beginning of the presentation. This is particularly understandable as we have just gone through quick introductions and curiosity prevails at this stage; the audience is eager to hear what you have to say. Anything that is new grabs people's attention and at the beginning of our demonstration, we are new to our audience: new faces, new voices, new styles, and hopefully new content. As presenters, we do not have to do anything to ignite attention in this stage; we simply need to properly leverage this initial but intense attention span and make the most out of it. Usually, this period of dedicated attention varies from five to ten minutes, with very few outliers having the ability to stay heavily focused for ten consecutive minutes.

- The attention span gradually corrodes throughout the presentation. Once the initial curiosity effect is over, attendees start paying less and less attention to your content; they have probably already formed an opinion of you and your sales partner, and if it's not stellar, it is an uphill battle from now on to get their interest back. This is when your audience starts looking at their phones or typing on their computers to answer emails. Not necessarily because you are not intriguing them enough with your demonstration, but because naturally the human mind needs to shift topics at constant intervals of time. This happens to all of us when focusing on something important for a good 20 minutes, and then the common interjection comes in: "I need a quick break." Well, your audience is experiencing the same when they listen to you, but for obvious reasons, they cannot ask for a break every 20 minutes. The result? They naturally tend to check out and divert their attention from you to something different to check back in later on, with a reduced level of interest and focus. Unfortunately, this low level of attention is experienced throughout the central part of the demonstration, which typically is the part consisting of the longest duration. For a good 35-40 minutes of your presentation, you might very well be talking to a distracted or un-focused audience.

- Towards the end of the presentation is usually when interest is re-ignited, and people start paying attention again. This often happens when words like "in conclusion" or "to recap" are used, and the reason is self-explanatory: your audience sees this moment as a way for them to catch up and take something away from the presentation with little effort. Especially after drawn-out demonstrations, the end of a presentation is always a moment where your attendees check back in. People put down their phones, move their chairs closer to the table, assuming a more erect position, or simply clear their voice while nodding. While this is a moment of high attention, it is typically not as intense as it was at the beginning of the presentation, when probably everybody was tuned in and listening to your words. Generally, this moment of increased, high attention from your audience lasts around three to five minutes and is followed by the official end of the meeting.

Let's now try to understand how we typically leverage the average attention curve illustrated above during a customer's meeting.

Common sense would tell us to take advantage of the highest moments of attention to deliver our key messages and elaborate on the key values our prospective customers will be benefitting from with our solution. Similarly, we should try to constantly re-ignite our audience's focus during any moments of low-level attention. The reality is most of us do not do this.

Here is what the great majority of Sales and Presales teams do during a typical sales meeting:

STAGE	ATTENTION LEVEL	POINTS MADE
Beginning (first 10-15 minutes)	Very High	Corporate Overview
Middle (40-50 minutes)	Fairly Low	Product Demo
End (5-10 minutes)	Fairly High	Q&A and Next Steps

Table 2.5.1. Message Delivered based on Attention Curve

If the last demo meeting you sat in followed a similar approach to what is depicted above, there is no doubt you are not properly leveraging the attention curve of your audience.

It is very common to start a presentation with the typical Corporate Overview deck that explains the foundations of your company, your mission, customer base, etc. All of this information is important, but it's just simply delivered at the wrong time!

Exactly like John Care noted in *Mastering Technical Sales. The Sales Engineer's Handbook*, right at the beginning, when you have the highest peak of attention, curiosity, and interest from your audience, you are trying to sell them something you cannot sell: your company, your customer base, or the market trends you explained on slide 18. You are just bombarding your audience with information they probably already know; the very same information they can easily gather independently on the web or learn themselves by reading the deck you will send them by email anyways.

Additionally, you may be presenting the same way your competitors did the day before, with the same approach and the same tool (PowerPoint deck) but probably with different formatting and logos. This does not scream differentiation and does not take advantage of the high-focused audience you have in front of you at the beginning of your meeting.

People are naturally selfish and want to hear how you will help them have better lives. Leverage those early minutes when no-one is looking at their phones to make it about them and not about you, your company, or your product.

Start with a "Why." Explain to your audience why you are meeting with them today.

Talk to them about their issues, show them you have done your homework, and give them solutions or different angles to approach their current must-haves. The most effective way to do this is to kick off the presentation with a quick ten-minute demo right after the introduction that, at a high level, hits on all of their points right away.

Without wasting their time on boring company decks, this approach will surprise your audience and will set you apart from the competition.

The only potential downside? Not adequately preparing for your ten-minute, value-selling product demonstration.

The middle chunk of your presentation is typically when the demo happens. Depending on the type of solution you are demoing, this could go from 30 minutes to several hours. Now that you are showing what you truly want to sell them, you have to fight with a low level of interest and an increased chance for distraction.

The way to fix it is to re-ignite your audience with interest and curiosity by breaking your presentation into multiple chunks so that their attention curve will look more like this:

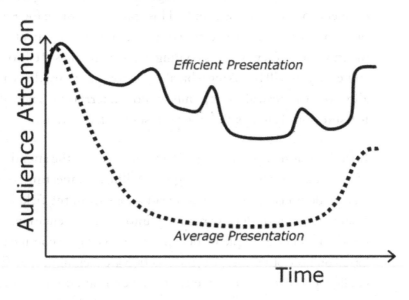

Figure 2.5.3. Optimal Attention Curve

As the image above shows, an efficient presentation is one that can keep the audience engaged by following these simple recommendations:

- Break your demo into mini-demos. Instead of talking non-stop for 30 minutes, break your presentation flow into logical topics of no more than 10-12 minutes each that will introduce, demo, recap, and ask for questions. A good example of this would be to go back to the Company Overview right after the initial high-level demo described in the previous paragraph. Moving your company presentation to the first mini-digestible presentation block will allow you to still make all the relevant points about your organization while keeping your audience curious enough to get back to the product demonstration.

- Tell your audience what is coming. By mentioning what you will be showing next, you will create anticipation and curiosity for your audience, who is now willing to wait for that moment. This goes well beyond the initial agenda that people forget the moment you go to the next slide. This approach is more focused on keeping your audience tuned-in and almost impatient by mentioning to them what is coming in a few minutes. Tell your audience you will be taking a break soon for questions; this will allow you to finish all your points without interruption and will reassure your listeners that they can soon ask questions.

- Include customer stories. A good way to revitalize the attention of your audience is by leveraging storytelling. Connecting your feature demonstration to real-life situations from the field is a smart way to introduce dynamicity into your presentation. A good customer example or best practice you can recommend based on how other users of your solution are tackling a specific challenge is always very effective to spike the attention of your listeners. Even better: if you're techy enough (and we know you are!), embed a quick customer testimonial video that is on point with your prospective customer's needs right in your presentation and play it live for your audience.

- Poll your audience. Polling is a powerful technique used to engage with your audience and is probably the most intrusive way of connecting with the public. In line with the therapist approach that quite often sales engineers are associated with, customers love expressing their opinions and being asked for their views on specific topics. Openly address your listeners by name and ask for their feedback or experience; this will allow for interaction during the product demonstration and will make the overall experience feel like an advisory session rather than just a marketing or sales meeting.

What is the main challenge of dynamic presentations? Change Management. Asking your sales partner to give up on the corporate overview at the beginning of the meeting might sound concerning or even scary. Thinking of breaking a product demonstration into mini-presentations—where not only do we show our solution, but we also present customer videos, market trends, best practices, and common pitfalls—is even revolutionary to some of Demo Gurus. The highest barrier to change is the status quo.

I am a firm believer of this dynamic approach to demos which constantly alternates feature selling to value selling, and I recommend you try it out at the beginning with some of your most seasoned sales partners. It requires some practice and refinement as it is for sure an uncommon, different approach, but I can guarantee you that you will be remembered.

The end of the presentation is when you typically can rely on a revitalized level of interest and attention from your listeners. This is when the audience is naturally inclined to tune back in to focus on what hopefully is the primary takeaway from the past 45 minutes.

Instead, I usually see the last few minutes of a customer's meeting focusing around the annoying question, "What's your next step?" First, asking this question at the end of a product demonstration shows a bigger problem that goes back to the initial pages of this handbook—lacking proper qualification and control of the sales cycle. Secondly, right when we have our entire audience's attention back on us, we don't want to come across as pushy salespeople that hope to close a transaction on the fly. Use the last five or ten minutes of your presentation to quickly summarize how you see your solution helping your audience, especially based on the experience and value from which many of their peers are already benefitting. Briefly go through any questions or topics you were not able to address, confirming they will get clarification the next day, and offer a follow up on any item for which they requested additional info. Do not be afraid of asking for feedback at this stage; on average, first impressions represent the most genuine and constructive criticism you can build on for your future meetings.

The attention curve is a standard behavioral concept on which all Sales Professionals should keep a close eye. Expanding the concept of *attention* to *retention* and ultimately to *learning* is where things get very interesting. Understandably enough, research has proven that what is usually presented during high peaks of attention is what is typically retained the most by any audience. What this means is that there is a direct correlation of *interest-attention-retention* of information. In other words, only what is of interest to your prospect will ignite his/her attention, and therefore it will be more likely that you will be remembered. Once again, this proves how critical it is to make sure we constantly talk about our customers' needs to pique their interest, making it about them, and how we have to do it at regular intervals to ensure we keep them constantly engaged with relevant content.

However, even if we dominate the attention and retention curve, this is not enough to seal the deal! Research proves that information is only processed and absorbed over the course of time. What that means is that you are not done the moment your demo is over! For your prospects to translate information to learned facts, they will need clarifications and repetitions. Still leveraging Gibbs' work on how to improve the quality of students' learning, it takes time and practice for a student (aka our prospective customers) to process the proposed information and learn:

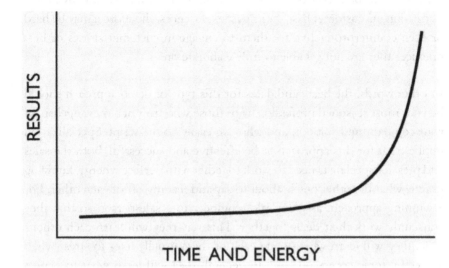

Figure 2.5.4. Typical Learning Curve

What this means for presales and sales professionals is that the work continues after Demo Day! The sales and presales teams must stay on top of their target client with timely follow-ups and use ABM (Account-Based Marketing) techniques that tend to position, clarify, and educate the prospect with relevant content at constant periods. Not that often are we lucky enough to close a deal after just one quick demo in the world of enterprise software sales!

 **Recommendation:**

Properly taking advantage of the attention curve is instrumental to the success of any presentation. Specifically, in the case of product demonstrations, the ability to break the main demo into mini-sessions could be a great differentiating point for you and your sales team. The biggest struggle is learning how to do this well, which requires two main factors: deep knowledge and high team specialization.

Deep knowledge refers to the fact that it would be hard for a relatively junior sales engineer or a recently hired salesperson to be effective with this approach. Maybe they are not yet entirely familiar with the company DNA, its mission, its customer base, or its past experiences, therefore it may be hard or even counterproductive for them to engage in customer stories or best practices they are not yet able to fully elaborate on.

In other words, the best candidates for this type of demo approach should be your most seasoned professionals or those who truly act as evangelists of your company and solution and who can easily go off-script. Specialization implies that for this approach to be effective and successful, both the sales and presales specialists need to work together with perfect synergy, knowing exactly what the other one is about to say and feeding off of each other. For a winning approach, assign a sales engineer to a salesperson so that they constantly work their deals together. This way they will learn each other's style, they will learn what points each of them usually likes to stress when a specific topic comes up, and, in general, they will learn what to expect from each other based on the situation they are facing. This will give them confidence to break their demonstrations into off-script chunks as they will already know what to expect from each other, how to use each other's content and points to seamlessly alternate focus, and how to exhibit flawless harmony to the customers.

 Top 3 Takeaways:

Remember the Attention Curve to...	
#1	Abandon the Corporate Overview at the beginning of your meeting and focus instead on what you can actually sell your audience when you have their highest attention.
#2	Break your presentation in smaller chunks, alternating presenters, types of content, and format to keep the audience constantly engaged.
#3	Translate from attention to learning in an effort to have your engaged audience retain the information you have shared with them.

Now that we have the basics down when it comes to establishing connections with any audience, let's go more in depth and analyze how to connect with a few specific personas:

- The C-Level

- The End User

- The Hostile User

- The Quiet User

- The Decision Maker

The C-level Connection

Top executives or senior management refer to a group of high-ranked individuals within an organization with comprehensive knowledge and exceptional leadership skills that set the strategy for the company and ensure its execution.

Dealing with C-level executives is not an easy task; normally, these individuals are dedicated to continuous improvement, expect solutions, hate whining, have high expectations, and love to be in charge—all while being extremely impatient given their packed schedules.

It is very unusual for chief officers to stay for the entire length of your presentation. Most of the time, senior executives come at the very beginning or join the rest of the team at the end of the demonstration for the final considerations, which is in line with the attention curve.

C-level crowds also like talking to their peers. If you know (and you should know) there will be executives attending your meeting, ask any of your company's most senior executives to join you for the presentation; it will add credibility and sponsorship to the meeting, and it will make your customer's executives feel important, appreciated, and recognized.

<u>With C-level Executives:</u>

- Ask about their personal views on the project. Top executives are usually very confident people that know exactly where they want to go and what they want to achieve, so it is advisable to openly seek their feedback on what the goal of this initiative should be. Most likely their broader statement will encompass process improvement and overall benefits for the entire organization and its customers and stakeholders, rather than selfish or emotionally-biased benefits.

- Focus on the bigger picture. Forget about the details or the exceptions and focus on the overall message by staying away from unnecessary outliers that C-level executives are not interested in. Focus on how your solution will help their business advance and the return they will be getting from investing in your solution. Make it quick with precise and factual statements that always leave room for them to interject at the end of your statement.

- Explain how your company operates. Executives expect your solutions to work, and most of the time they are less interested in *how* it works for them and more in how *you* work with them as an organization. They typically rely on their assistants to make sure your solution ticks all the boxes and meets all of their most detailed requirements. What they will want to evaluate themselves is how your organization will be doing business with them. Make sure you spend a couple of minutes explaining how your company will guide theirs to success, how you will be able to support them throughout this important initiative, and how you will be partnering with them throughout the entire journey. This type of audience is usually more interested in the thought process behind any request than the actual request itself; therefore, explaining how your organization operates in similar circumstances can be an area of interest for many C-level executives.

- Finish ahead of time. Do not count on the whole allotted time the executives have agreed to dedicate to you. Not only are their agendas extremely busy, but they are also extremely flexible; emergencies or out-of-schedule matters pop up regularly for top executives, requiring their immediate attention. Show you understand their situation and are thankful for the time they have given you by finishing your presentation a few minutes before schedule. This approach will set you apart from the great majority of the executive meetings that rarely finish before schedule and will contribute to that memorable experience you want your entire audience to have when you meet them.

- Practice your value pitch. Always be prepared to answer this fatal question: "I only have one minute; tell me what your company does and why it's better than your competitors." There is no time for jokes here and there is no need for tasteless selling. You have to be to the point and address your executive's question with confidence and precision, making it about the value his or her team will be getting by partnering with your organization. Practice the C-level value pitch ahead of time to make sure you are not caught unprepared.

True Story: The Pilot Analogy

During one of my latest presentations, when everything was proceeding smoothly with my audience, a person stepped into the meeting, asking us to go ahead as he quietly took a seat. I obeyed his instructions and kept going for maybe less than ten minutes when the gentleman interrupted with a sudden question: "Are you sure this will be a success for me?" Completely off-guard, I asked him first who he was (in a much more polite way than that just came across!) The quiet man who entered the room insisting on not interrupting happened to be the founder of the $2.1 billion organization to which we were presenting. I answered the question by saying I could not be sure of any outcome, just like I was not sure I would fly back home that night without any issues. But just like my pilot would try to find the safest route to fly, with maybe a few bumps here and there, I explained to the quiet disruptor that I would take the same approach with him and his team. We, as an organization, would be there with his team throughout the journey to take care of the bumps that inevitably will be experienced, with the ultimate goal to take them to the end of it safely. The rest of the presentation was on how we both were on the same boat (or plane!) and how we should collaborate as partners for our mutual benefit.

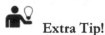 **Extra Tip!**

C-Level executives usually appreciate meeting their peers from other organizations. Even if just you, the Demo Guru, and your sales counterpart attended the actual meeting where an Executive was present from the customer side, it is always advisable to have a similar level from your organization reach out after the meeting. Not someone from the Sales organization, but preferably your CFO/CEO or Head of Customer Success should send a quick note or even a LinkedIn request to connect. Chances are that your C-level connection will engage!

The End User Connection

"End Users" is a very common expression that addresses a very specific category of software users. With this term, we typically refer to the business users that will be implementing a solution or will be leveraging a specific service to satisfy the usual requirements and challenges that their daily job brings to them.

Depending on the type of solution or service you are providing, end users could have a huge impact on the buying cycle of any organization and therefore need ultimate attention. This is particularly true in the area of cloud solutions, which make the products or services you are providing much more accessible and less of an initial substantial investment as opposed to legacy on-premise solutions that require considerable upfront investments.

Coupled with the ever-increasing collaborative approach organizations have across their teams, business users are nowadays a key target we should learn how to connect with.

End users are completely different from C-level users. They are usually more interested in their specific issues and how their lives can improve with your solutions and services. Maybe they do not have full visibility in the overall situation, strategy, or mission of the entire organization like the C-level does, and for this reason, business users are usually more "selfish" and less interested in how your solution will affect the overall well-being of the organization as long as it can make their own lives better.

Expect to go into excruciating details with these types of users; do not be surprised if they ask you to proof even the most basic requirements you would take for granted, and be patient if they talk to you using industry acronyms and terminology like you have been an employee of their company for the last 20 years.

The discovery call is a vital exercise to effectively connect with your end users; in that meeting, you will learn about their most annoying frustrations and what their perfect world would look like. This will give you a chance to empathize with them during your demo, showing them you know what they are going through.

True Story: Focusing on the Wrong Persona

This is a story where I actually lost a deal to one of our competitors but still a good example of end user connection. I was doing this presentation for a technology company in Rhode Island. This was a very competitive sales opportunity with many vendors bidding for the business. We met with a few people, but our main point of contact was Mike (obviously a fictitious name), a business user who had been with the company for almost 35 years. Mike was the single source of truth for the entire organization; everybody went to Mike when they needed help. Mike was so proud of his work that he escorted me and my team twice to see his server room; an impeccable maze of wires and cables that looked like a spaceship only Mike had a key for. Of course, my solution had nothing to do with the server room as we were not selling hardware. Still, that quick trip to the server room made our user feel important and finally appreciated for all the hard work he'd put in that his co-workers were not acknowledging. As much as Mike liked us and was sponsoring our solution, unfortunately, it was not enough to seal the deal as we had completely missed the political map of that buying process.

With End Users:

- Acknowledge their challenging job and demanding bosses, especially in front of their top management team. It is always rewarding for them and respectful of you to recognize the hard work the end users are in charge of, with usually thousands of questions coming their way and limited time to prepare. I am not recommending to have an agenda item for your meeting to formally address how fantastic the end users of the organization you are demoing to are; rather, I am suggesting making a point subtly during your presentation. The business users will feel you are on their side and, more importantly, they now have an external, third-party ally that understands their challenges.

- Let them vent but reassure them. Even in the best world possible, people will still complain about something. Listen to your end users' complaints and their frustrations with their job, the usual last second requests from their management, and their late nights at the office to get it all done; but most importantly, reassure them. Have them understand they are not alone, that it happens everywhere, and that you have seen the same situation in many of the organizations that call you for help. It's why you are there, and you have fixed that same situation for many of your customers.

- Make them feel important. This is probably one of the most ignored factors in connecting with these types of users. The people doing all of the hard work—which is then shared with somebody else—feel like they are the ones that are making the difference but no one seems to notice it. Think of how many times in your career you have prepared a research paper or an analysis for your boss who then went to the board and presented your exact findings without giving you credit for it. Your job as part of the sales team is to make sure everybody loves you. Make your end users feel they are not left behind but that they instead have a key responsibility for the success of your product or service as they will be the ones making it work. If you are planning a business lunch with their top executives, plan two: one where the end users will be attending and another one for a restricted audience. If you are unsure, ask for their opinion during your presentation; seeking their engagement and inputs makes them feel you value their views and are genuinely interested in their opinions just as much as you are interested in their boss's perspective.

- Talk their language: Probably the most important aspect when you are presenting to end users is that they see you as a knowledgeable subject matter expert that knows about their business and has ideas on how to help them. Talk about their business in detail, address them by name, use their product naming, bring up use cases, and make them wish they had you on their team.

The Hostile User Connection

As non-disruptive as you view your solution or service to be, it will still represent some change to which the overall organization and its people will have to adapt. Especially if change implies taking some people out of their comfort zone, you will have to learn how to deal with a few individuals in your meeting that might not fully be on your side.

There are multiple reasons why during a demo you might encounter users with a pre-conceived perception of your solution or product; these users are typically very conservative, risk-averse, or simply love their status quo, no matter what the best course of action is for their company.

Hostile users might present themselves in very interesting shapes and formats. Maybe you are dealing with some users that have worked for several years with one of your major competitors and therefore have established a personal relationship with another vendor.

Maybe you are trying to position your products and services to a newly hired individual that has prior experience confidently using a competitor's product and does not want to risk his or her first assignment. Or, way more simply, your competition has done a much better job than you and has seeded many concerns into your prospect's mind, and you are now struggling to defeat them.

The most challenging type of hostile users, however, are those that do not manifest their hostility and are the hardest to decipher. No comments, neither good nor bad, and no emotions; just a very professional "Thank you for your time today" is all you can plan to get from these types of hostile users.

True Story: Let's Get It Out!

For the great majority of my career, I have been working for a European-based software company that decided to come over to the US and penetrate the Corporate Performance Management market there. While in the US, I took the responsibility of their Presales department, actively involving myself in many presentations. During an onsite presentation to a law firm in the Philadelphia area, I had one of the users first ask me about local resources available for the implementation of our solution. A few minutes later, the same user asked me about language support, then about our local competency center, still not openly admitting his concern of dealing with a European-based corporation. Finally, the most evident but still indirect question came up, asking where they would call in case they needed after-hours live support. Even though I knew exactly where that user was going since the first question, I waited a bit longer to address the elephant in the room: "Yes, we are a European-based company, and I know that our competition says we have no local, English-speaking resources to help you. I am local, and I am Italian; try calling our US support line right now and see who answers the phone." After a few laughs, the hostile user thanked me for addressing his concern, and the trust I gained by simply stating the facts set the tone for the rest of the presentation.

No matter what format the hostile user comes in, it is fundamental to prepare for this type of prospective customer and have a well-defined strategy on how to either attack them or win them over. Too many times, we finish up our demo and high-five with our account executives because we got so much good feedback during the presentation by so many users, but we forget about those attendees that instead did not show any emotion. Focusing on who likes us is easy and rewarding; focusing on who does not like us is a hard necessity that requires seasoned talent.

<u>With Hostile Users:</u>

- Address the elephant in the room. The typical signal that it is now time to address a specific issue is when your hostile users quietly ask you questions that subtly but elegantly aim to expose a potential issue of your solution or product. Instead of leaving it unaddressed, which could create additional confusion and make the entire team, not just the hostile user, preoccupied and even fearful, address the concern in a manner that makes the conversation productive and leaves the entire team comfortable with your answer. By calling out and naming the exact issue to which your hostile user is referring, you will transform an issue into an opportunity for everybody to get clarity. Be honest and direct when you make your points, even if they might be unpleasant, and stick to facts with assertion. Tiptoeing on half-truth will only reinforce your hostile user's position.

- Sit next to your dissenters. This is probably the technique I use most frequently when I am aware of hostile users attending my presentation. Again, the importance of the pre-demo work from the discovery call to the political map is of extreme relevance to effectively do this. Physically aligning with your opponents or constantly asking for their feedback and thoughts during a web presentation shows great confidence first, but more importantly, it shows openness to dialogue. Mingling with your dissenters will reduce the gap between you and them and will make them feel you are sincerely considering their objections.

- Confront the negatives in the room. I like to think that customers are always right until they are blatantly wrong. At that point, it is my chance to react professionally and constructively. Very hostile users sometimes might come up with irrational and even contradictory reasons just for the sake of avoiding your company or products. When that happens, it is your duty to respectfully disagree. In most cases, by factually stating your opponent's point and humbly explaining your view, you will disarm the hostile user (who will now be less inclined to be vocal about any other opinionated statements).

- Capitalize on the common ground. In a situation where some fair and healthy friction has already occurred between you and your hostile users, it is critical to look for areas where you both share the same view and bring them up in the conversation. If masterfully done, anytime you expect there will be disagreements with your audience on some upcoming topics, it is wiser to bring up those common views earlier in the meeting. With this strategy in mind, the hostile user will feel less negativity towards you during your presentations as some common ground has already been established.

Extra Tip!

Do not be intimidated by Hostile Users. Typically, the reasons why users may show hostile behaviors is that they are intimidated by you and specifically by the change that you are presenting to them. Embrace the hostility and deal with it once the demo is over. A quick private email the day after your presentation offering a follow up session just to your hostile users will make them feel valuable and at least will intrigue them to learn more about your solution.

The Quiet User Connection

Have you ever demoed to a bunch of statues that sometimes even you wonder if your phone line is still alive? If you have, I am sure you are familiar with that feeling of pulling teeth when you are trying to get your audience to ask questions, provide feedback, or simply even answer any question you are asking with a bit more articulation than a simple head nod.

These types of users are, without a doubt, some of the most complicated types of audiences to interact with, and the reason is exactly because of that: lack of interaction. It is hard to gauge if what you are saying is of interest to them, let alone how you are doing.

You are trying hard to get your audience engaged by constantly polling them, asking if what you are showing relates to them, but all you are getting is some passive indication or acknowledgment without any further action. It is not easy to reinvigorate people in these types of audiences. You want to be sensitive to their personalities and professional enough not to push or embarrass any of them or accidentally expose what they are not comfortable with.

There are, however, a few techniques that can shake things up a bit to encourage increased participation without being perceived as too pushy.

<u>With Quiet Users:</u>

- Ask open-ended questions. If all you are getting is a quick yes or no to your questions, try to ask questions that require more articulation. For example, instead of asking if whether the feature that you have just demonstrated applies to their business, ask them how that same feature could be utilized in the context of their company. This way your audience will feel morally compelled to not simply answer the question but also provide a bit more context to at least show they have been following the presentation.

- Call for a quick break. Chances are that your amenable audience will agree to that. If this is an onsite demonstration, between you and your AE, try to reach out to any of the attendees while having coffee and establish some casual conversation. When the time is right, ask for feedback and guidance. Typically, when engaged separately, quiet users tend to be less quiet and more vocal. If instead this is a web demo, wait for your audience to come back from the break and, right before resuming your demonstration, ask them if what you have shown so far lives up to their expectations. Most importantly, openly ask them what they want to see next. Do not be afraid of losing time to ask for a break because you still have many topics to cover. You have no idea if what you have been saying so far is in line with their expectations anyways. You might as well take a pause and get your thoughts together, ensuring the information is as relevant to your audience as possible.

- As a last resort, have your audience understand you are experiencing some hard times gauging your effectiveness in this presentation. Sentences like "I will keep going for a while now, but please interrupt me anytime if you have a question" serve that purpose. The audience will feel relieved you are not checking in on them every two minutes and will feel it is on them now to make themselves heard.

Silence is not automatically a bad sign! At some point, despite all of your attempts to establish some kind of contact with your quiet users, all you can do is believe that you are doing great until you hear otherwise! And sometimes that nice call from your sponsor right after the demo proves just that: you did much better than you thought!

Extra Tip!

Being mindful of different cultures and geographies, contemplate doing something unusual during your presentation to shake things up. I have witnessed presentations where the sales person positioned a container in the middle of the conference table and asked the quiet audience to take 5 minutes to write whatever feedback or question they had on a piece of paper and enter it anonymously in the container. Similarly, and quite successfully, I have been part of full-day demo meetings where on the main door of the conference room, attendees were adding post-it notes with their requests between one break and another!

The Decision Maker Connection

The need for establishing a relationship with those that will be signing the contract does not require any explanation. What instead requires intensive study, research, and preparation is finding out who will be signing the contract, which is usually a task your account executive will be in charge of.

Depending on the industry you operate in and the products or services you provide, the decision-making process could vary considerably.

In the enterprise software industry, for instance, the buying process has changed dramatically in the past few years due to two main reasons. First, SaaS technologies have made software solutions more "affordable" and therefore less risky, which in turn allowed for the delegation of purchase power to line managers instead of the C-level executives, who get involved just towards the end of the buying cycle. Secondly, there has been a shift in power from the vendor side to the buyer side, which is now a well-educated purchaser and requires more from its vendors than ever before.

So while it's still true that the final blessing will be given by a C-level executive, in the SaaS business, it is more and more common that top management will rely mostly on what their teams will recommend to them. The decision maker, in this case, is therefore not an individual person with a high-sounding title, but a collaborative committee where business line managers have a big influence.

Connecting with the decision makers requires focusing on the mix of the three profiles described above. My recommendation when delivering a demo is to keep in mind that any person attending your presentation could influence the decision-making process, so every attendee requires maximum attention and dedication. Right after your presentation, a quick recap email should be sent to the entire team to thank them for their time and should list the top five "wow moments" that your attendees experienced during your presentation, addressing the needs of both executives, end users, and dissenters.

While on one side we are horizontally treating the entire team as the "decision maker," it is fundamental to vertically analyze that same team in relation to the culture, politics, and direction of the organization to make sure we account for "stronger voices" in that group. We might find out, for instance, that the top executive of the firm to which we are demoing has a preference for a certain provider he or she did some business with in the past.

No matter who you have identified your decision maker to be for your specific sale—either the selection committee as a whole or the CEO of the entire organization—when connecting with them, you and your account executive need to demonstrate direction and control. Direction refers to the ability to show how the process will unfold considering the initiative they are embarking on; in other words, what happens next (reference checking, contract red-lining, project start date, etc.) Control refers to giving your decision makers visibility into the status of each step you have outlined to them, keeping them accountable for their tasks and explaining consequences for missed due dates.

 **Recommendation:**

You must ask your account executive to identify the decision maker before you jump into any demonstration. As discussed, this is not an easy task and requires a lot of research into the political map of the organization; this is, however, no excuse for lack of detailed due diligence. As a seasoned sales engineer with a considerable win rate, you should make no exceptions to this. By knowing who will be making the final decision, you can focus your resources during the demo on the proper target and increase your chances of selling successfully.

How to Re-engage Your Audience

It happens to all professional presenters that at some point in time, especially during extended presentations, the audience might disconnect and lose interest in what you are discussing.

Humans are, by definition, social and interactive creatures; standing still for a long time watching someone else run the show, or even worse, listening for long periods to presenters discussing topics of little relevance to them, could be a challenge.

Neurology also poses a threat to focus and concentration: our brains are constantly on the lookout for additional information and inputs. No new stimulation means our brains will be searching for something different to simply stay occupied.

True Story: Who Is in for Some Hands-on Experience?

The most recent global pandemic has not made it any easier for Demo Gurus to judge the quality of their work during a presentation. Without an easy way to assess your audience's reactions, you need to rely on their active participation and eagerness to ask questions. Very recently, I was part of a web demonstration to a team of ten attendees. At the very beginning, they were all very engaged. Everybody activated their camera for intros and even asked multiple questions while reviewing the goal of the presentation. Just a few minutes after the demonstration started, the audience changed completely and my sales engineer struggled to get any participation. No matter how hard he tried to get their feedback, we could barely get any comments or interaction until he passed the control of the screen and asked the most vocal attendee to use the software live with him. My sales engineer was able to change his delivery mode right on the fly, made it about the customer, and got them to drive. Even though this was just for a few minutes, all the other attendees started participating more actively in the meeting and volunteered for some remote, hands-on participation during the remainder of the presentation.

There are two main proof points that we have lost our audience and need to shift things around immediately: cell phone use and yawning. If the same person is looking at his or her phone while yawning at the same time, then that is a really bad sign!

How can we fix that?

- **Ask for a break.** If possible, ask your audience if they would like to take a five-minute break. Most often, just standing up and taking a quick walk back to the desk can re-invigorate people who then come back to the session, especially if it is a long one, with a rejuvenated attention span. This option applies only when your audience is fairly small, say a group of 10 or maximum 13 people, and is effective both in case of onsite, physical presentations, or remote web demonstrations.

In case of larger audiences, for instance, a keynote or a plenary session at a conference, the topic itself and the usually limited duration of these presentations should be the drivers to keep your audience engaged to begin with, along with the presenter's passionate tone and appealing style.

- <u>Seek user participation.</u> Probably the easiest way to grab someone's attention is to address that person directly, even by name, if possible. When you see yourself losing steam with your audience, try bringing them back into the conversation by asking for their opinions on the subject you are presenting. This could be done in countless ways, both with larger and smaller crowds. Show of hands is a quick and standard way to get user participation in the case of larger audiences. I have personally attended a conference where the presenter was pooling her audience by asking them to stand up; it was a smart way to induce movement and action in the audience, keeping them awake throughout the presentation.

- <u>Change mode of delivery.</u> This is not just referring to changing your tone of voice, your pace, or the energy you show during a presentation, nor is this referring to the obvious change of position from sitting down to standing up or moving left to right on the stage. Changing the delivery mode might also imply alternating presentation tools. During a demonstration, try to alternate your software presentation with a few PowerPoint slides to bring home the points you just demonstrated, or play a quick video of a customer story that is similar to the prospect's situation. Using digital assets, such as customer video testimonials or real-life examples in the forms of screenshots of how other customers are using your products or services, is a phenomenal way to break the boredom of someone speaking for hours, no matter how engaging the presenter is.

Chapter 2.6 – Calling All Demo Gurus

In this chapter, we will examine some key fundamentals that every Sales Engineer should either naturally possess or diligently develop and some basic best practices useful even to the most seasoned professionals. From proper question handling to verbal and non-verbal skills, we will be highlighting the preferred behaviors to assume depending on some of the most common situations Demo Gurus find themselves in.

The Basics of Question Handling

Hopefully, your presentation is not a lecturing monologue but rather an interactive and engaging conversation with your audience. What this means is that your audience will be inevitably asking questions.

Some of the questions you will like, as they play along with your product or your demo flow, and some others not so much, as they might expose weaknesses of your solution or represent a disruption to your demo script. There are hundreds of papers and seminars on question management, which all confirm one main concept: answering questions is not an easy task for any presenter.

Before deep-diving into the recommended behavioral approach for each type of question we might receive during a presentation, let's first review a few basic concepts of Question Handling that we should all keep in mind when responding to any inquiry.

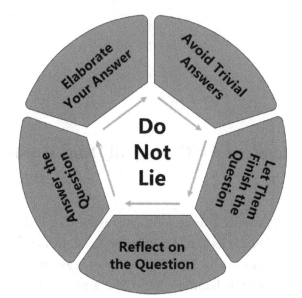

Figure 2.6.1. Basics of Question Handling

- Avoid the usually hyper-inflated "That's a great question" comment or its conventionally abused sister-filler "I am so glad you asked," unless what your audience is asking is truly remarkable and exceptional. Many presenters fall in the habit of answering any question with praise for the question asked, no matter its value or originality, just as a technique to gain a few useful seconds to put their thoughts together. Treat your audience as seasoned professionals and gratify their interaction when there is an evident need to do so.

- Answer the question you have been asked, not what you want to answer. This does not apply only to presentations but to many other areas that involve social interaction. From job interviews to simple everyday conversations, we are all naturally inclined to respond by immediately relaying what we are proud of and what our comfort zone pushes us towards. Address the question clearly at the beginning and expand as necessary only once your audience has received the answer they were expecting.

- Have your audience finish their question, even if you know the answer already. We are all human beings and we all have emotions. When we know where our prospect is heading, we are naturally inclined to jump in, finish the sentence on their behalf, and start answering their question. Keep those emotions under control and give your prospect their moment of glory. Attentively listen to their question through to the end and let yourself go only once the audience member has finished his or her thought.

- The first question is usually the least important for the audience. You have just started your presentation and a few minutes in, you have a question from your audience. Typically, the first to ask a question is seldom the end user of your solution or the analyst or the Project Management Organization (PMO) running the evaluation. Most often, the one that breaks the ice is a high-profile individual in the customer organization. C-level executives asking questions right at the beginning of the presentation usually have two main objectives: invite their team members to be interactive with the presentation and, more importantly, test how you address their question. There is traditionally little value for the prospect in the first question they ask you, and usually the goal of the first question is to assess your style, your personality, and your overall attitude towards question handling.

- Elaborate your answers at the beginning of your presentation to gain trust. As much as we want to establish ourselves as trusted advisors and subject matter experts, anytime we jump into a meeting to showcase our solutions and product, we are perceived as selling. One of the best opportunities for you to gain trust from your audience is by responding to your prospect's question to the point and immediately expanding on your answer with customer stories, additional features, and best practices or experiences from the field in the first 30 minutes of your presentation. This will allow you to gain your audience's trust and could also come in handy later on during the presentation when they ask you a hostile question you do not want to spend too much time on. At this point, with the trust you've built, you will be in a position to simply answer with a YES, likely without having to expand on it, relying on the expertise and credibility you have established at the beginning of the demonstration.

- Don't lie. Lying is easily the worst mistake you could do even as a seasoned Demo Guru. Most likely you will be presenting your solutions or products to people that on one side do not know anything about your offering; on the other side, those same people will be able to tell when something sounds suspicious. Making up an answer just for the sake of providing one could damage your credibility and trustworthiness, which are the top qualities you want to continuously build on with your audience. Amplifying a concept, maybe even stretching into areas that are not completely available in your solution, might be possible and safe as long as you know that what you are indirectly committing to is doable and you are not misleading your audience. Even if you are the best poker player in the world, the odds of your audience perceiving you like cheating on them are way too high and not worth your reputation.

Types of Questions

By now, we all understand we will have to change our behavior and our strategy when answering questions depending on the exact request.

Based on my experience in enterprise software selling, I have identified five different types of questions our prospects' inquiries typically fall into: the good question, the hostile question, the competitive question, the useless question, and the "I don't know the answer" question.

- **The GOOD question.** This type of question fits right in with your demo flow or product strengths and differentiators and is exactly in line with what you are about to show next or the point you are about to make. Just as if you had a sidekick planted in the audience, not only do we love these questions because they naturally lead to our next screen, but they give us a chance to answer the prospect's request immediately and most importantly, "naturally."

  The key to answering these questions is to address them right away, right to the point, and build on them as you see your prospect gaining more and more interest in your answer. One problem you may face when answering these questions is that you do not let your prospect finish the question because you already know exactly how you want to respond. Show respect and let them finish their thoughts before jumping into your answer.

GOOD QUESTIONS	
Do This:	**Don't Do This:**
Answer the question right away, right to the point, and build on demand	Cut off your audience in the excitement of replying to a question you know the answer to

- **The HOSTILE question.** Statistically, for every three to five good questions we get asked, chances are we get one not-so-good question that one way or the other we have to address. Hostile questions are tricky questions that either derail your demo flow or show a product weakness. Surprisingly enough, these questions are easier to answer and by far less intimidating than most would think.

If they simply tend to create a problem for your demo flow because it is not "the right time" to address that question, simply park it. Parking a question is a phenomenal way to have your audience understand you will certainly address their request but at a different point in the presentation. In this scenario, it is fundamental that you openly and confidently state to your audience that you will take a note of the question and answer it later in the demonstration. If your sales counterpart is in the room with you, call his or her name publicly and ask him/her to take note; otherwise, do it yourself on a piece of paper, a sticky note on your virtual desktop, or a whiteboard. Do take note of the question you are parking as it will show your audience you are not simply dodging their request but seriously postponing it. And even more seriously, remember to answer any questions you have parked on the whiteboard before you leave the room.

If the hostile question is exposing a weakness of your solution, the situation is more delicate. As an evangelist for your company and within your company, if you find your prospects asking the same hostile question multiple times, it is probably a good idea to talk to your product management team to investigate what kind of development or solution can be put in place to address that hostile request. In the meantime, however, you will still need to answer it. Be as confident and brief with your answer as you can, and focus on storytelling more than ever, even if that implies explaining to your customer how your solution roadmap is considering enhancing that area of your solution in the near term. Emphasize the vision and the value of your programmed enhancement rather than focusing on a current weakness that could jeopardize the overall perception of your solution. Typically, parking a hostile question will allow you to briefly touch back on it towards the end of the presentation—after you have already established your credibility—and focus more on value selling without exposing a weakness in your solution.

HOSTILE QUESTIONS	
Do This:	**Don't Do This:**
Park them if you can and focus on value selling, explaining upcoming enhancements and remaining calm, courteous, and empathetic	Have them derail your flow or even your entire presentation just for the sake of answering right away

- **The COMPETITIVE question.** I love it when my prospects ask me *"So, how do you compare your solution to XYZ?"* where XYZ is one of my main competitors. These questions allow me to build credibility with my audience, while at the same time landing some mines in my competitors' field. We have already discussed how we should, subtly but professionally, allude to some known short-fallings of our competition during the actual demonstration. In this case, however, you have been openly asked to provide feedback on a specific competitor, and your approach should be different depending on the competitor you have been asked to comment on:

  o If the competitor is in reality a non-direct-competitor, meaning an industry player with a different market segment or positioning, say so openly, quickly, and move on. Do not waste too many words on any player that is not a direct competitor of yours; simply state that the vendor is no competition for your solution and quickly explain why. In your explanation, do not focus on what they do worse in terms of features and functions, but focus on why they do not have the dignity to be considered a competitor of yours. This approach will be extremely effective as it will convince the prospect your solution is on a different level.

  o If the competitor you need to comment on is one of your fiercest, acknowledge that and be prepared to focus on two or at a maximum three key areas of differentiation. Remember these areas could of course be specific features or lack thereof, but they could also extend to company viability, quality of the people, and management stability, or even quality of their customer support. Use analysts' reports and tap into all those slide decks that your Competitive Intelligence department has put together for you, but do not forget to search for public online reviews from current users of your competitors' offering.

No matter what approach you follow, there is one key element you must make clear with your prospective customer when explicitly talking about your competition: you are not an expert at your competitor's offering. Everything you have disclosed to them is based on your understanding of the competitor's solutions and product; it might be outdated, it might be incomplete, and it might even be incorrect. Be professional under any circumstance and never trash the competition. Conversely, openly invite your prospect to confirm everything you have mentioned to them about your competition directly with the opposing vendor, but most importantly ask your audience to do the same with you. Most likely your prospect will be asking the same question to your competitor about your solutions as well. Instead of having them simply rely on what a competitor tells them, invite them to confirm the information with you, just like you are encouraging them to confirm what you just said about your competition directly with them. This approach will boost your credibility and, above all, it will give you a chance to respond to any potential attacks from your competition.

COMPETITIVE QUESTIONS	
Do This:	**Don't Do This:**
State you are not an expert at your competitor's offering and invite your prospect to confirm your assumptions	Give too much attention to your non-direct competitors or, on the contrary, aggressively trash your direct competition

- **The "I DO NOT KNOW THE ANSWER" question.**
  It happens. It has happened to the best of us and, hopefully, it

will happen again in the future to many of us. Sometimes we are asked a question we do not know the answer to. The best way to address these types of questions is to openly admit you do not know the answer and clarify you will get back to them after some additional investigation. This will show you are an honest presenter and that you are taking their question very seriously. Do not make up an answer just for the sake of answering; wrong information is much worse than no information. There is nothing embarrassing in openly saying you do not know the answer to that question and need to do more research on it before getting back to them. On the contrary, it plays to your advantage as you gain credibility with your prospect. Instead of simply responding with a dubious "Yes" or, even worse, answering their question with a completely different answer, this will show your audience you have not been selling to them so far but have been "speaking the truth." Furthermore, professionally admitting a lack of knowledge with respect to the question you have just received inherently gives pride to the person who asked the question to start with.

"I DO NOT KNOW THE ANSWER" QUESTIONS	
Do This:	**Don't Do This:**
Openly state you do not know the answer to the question and commit to a follow-up	Make up an answer just for the sake of responding

- **The USELESS question.** Not all questions are great questions, yet useless questions by far give you a fabulous opportunity to establish your subject matter expertise. For some reason, certain people seem to take pleasure in stumbling the presenter. This typically happens when you are facing a customer that does not like you, your product, or your company, or because that person is simply not brilliant or is purely looking to show off.

The best way to address this type of question is by professionally challenging your audience. Ask them to give you an example of what instead they would like to see with the question they are asking. Most of the time, when they are put in a situation to rationally think about what they have just asked, they will end up with the typical "*I guess it does not matter.*" They have now just had their epiphany-moment and have fully recognized the uselessness of their question.

True Story: What Are You Talking About?

I will give you a real-life example of how effective professional push back is under this type of circumstance. I was giving a presentation to a small audience of no more than seven people, all with a heavy Finance background, talking about automatic double entry and debit/credit journals. Now, for the non-accountant readers of this chapter, double-entry bookkeeping was first invented by a Franciscan monk in Europe in the 15th century and it has not changed its fundamentals to this day, no matter what part of the world you are in! During my explanation of how our solution guaranteed perfect traceability by inherently supporting a double-entry logic, a member of the customer's selection committee dropped a USELESS question: "What if I wanted to come up with my own bookkeeping logic?" Being somewhat flabbergasted by the request, I asked this person to give me an example of what kind of alternative bookkeeping system he would like to adopt. And, of course, he let me continue my presentation with the usual "I guess it does not matter."

The most delicate aspect of dealing with useless questions is two-fold. First, there is a high risk of sounding arrogant, aggressive, or even "insulting" when pushing back. It is imperative to respond in a polite and extremely genuine way by showing your audience you do not want to diminish the importance of the question, but rather, you want to understand the request properly before responding. Second, and this mostly applies to relatively new Demo Gurus, there is a high chance of falling into the trap of beginning to answer the question that should have not been asked to begin with, with a potential loss of credibility. Rational and analytical thinking come in handy more than ever in this scenario to counterbalance the lack of logical thinking these types of questions naturally cause.

USELESS QUESTIONS	
Do This:	**Don't Do This:**
Genuinely and politely challenge your audience to rethink their question	Emotionally embrace the lack of logical thinking by answering useless questions anyway

- **The REAL question.** This is the question we should all be ready for; instead, most of the time, I see many presenters struggling to answer the question *"What is your solution's biggest weakness?"* All our marketing communication focuses on how our company and solutions are better than the competition. All our sales training materials focus on our solution's differentiators with battle-cards that teach us how to attack the competition. During a presentation, all our talking is mostly centered on why we are the best fit for our prospective customer's needs. In other words, we tend to believe that self-promotion is the ticket to success.

Yet, we all have our skeletons in the closets. It's just that we do not like to talk about them! Customers, however, especially the most interested ones, also want to know where we see ourselves struggling and how we plan to address our shortcomings.

This type of inquiry is usually a good sign, especially if you are receiving such a question right at the end of your demonstration by a C-level executive. This shows your audience is impressed with your work so much so that it almost seems "too good to be true".

Just like an interviewer during a candidate screening process, with REAL questions your audience wants to find out whether you can be open and forthcoming and whether you have a healthy level of self-awareness. Remember that your audience will not expect you or your products to be perfect; most likely, they have already conducted extensive research on your solution and are probably already aware of your market-perceived weaknesses.

When addressing these types of questions it is recommended to be on-point and as factual as possible to communicate awareness and share any upcoming mitigation strategy.

Start by clearly stating the weakness.

As usual, this requires preparation and practice. When admitting some kind of inadequacy of your solution to perform specific tasks, be authentic, and phrase your response to convey self-awareness and control. If possible and truthful, briefly discuss shortcomings that are not essential for your audience or low on their priority list. This will make them feel you are genuinely opening up with them but will also not worry them tremendously as the items you are mentioning will not impact them too much.

If instead, your solution's weakness is around a key area of interest for your new customer, briefly state so and move quickly to the mitigation plan to show what is currently being done to address and improve the situation.

Focus on the mitigation plan.

The main topic of discussion to address any REAL question should be how the current shortcomings will be fixed in the near future. Spend the time to explain how your organization is actively working on improving the weakness you have mentioned and bring examples of how this was also the case in the past. By demonstrating that previous weaknesses have been identified and corrected will increase your credibility as you are not shying away from mentioning past fragilities (remember your audience expects you and your product not to be perfect) and will show confidence that your organization knows how to handle this type of situations already.

True Story: Panic Mode

This story happened very recently to my A-Team during a demonstration to a Canadian manufacturing provider. As usual, the team prepares diligently for this meeting. Opportunity plan is in place, multiple strategy meetings are on the calendar to discuss roles, responsibilities, messages to be conveyed and of course, the political map is at the center of attention. The CFO will be attending. During Demo Day, while the meeting is in progress, I receive text messages from the account rep and my director of sales that the demonstration is going perfectly; lots of discussions, some product here and there, great engagement and interaction from the team. After almost three hours of presentation, the very vocal CFO asks the REAL question. My A-Team, who has been doing this for years, struggles to answer the question. Team members start cutting each other off just to throw their views fearing someone else could expose too much of our solution's weaknesses. The result was an uncoordinated and confusing response to a very basic question that instead requires conciseness, assertiveness, and situational control. Moral of the story? No one's perfect – not even your A-Team!

REAL QUESTIONS	
Do This:	**Don't Do This:**
Factually and briefly address any product shortcoming and focus the discussion on mitigation plans mentioning past successful examples of similar cases	Show denial by arrogantly claiming your solution has no weaknesses or go overboard by turning every weakness into a strength

Best Practices in Question Handling

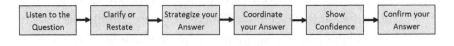

Figure 2.6.2. Best Practices Question Handling

We have already covered some high-level fundamentals of question management and discussed some clearly defined behaviors we recommend depending on the question we need to answer in the previous pages. Yet, there is much more to be said when it comes to proper question handling. Far from providing an exhaustive framework for question handling, the following are some best practices that apply to any question we are asked to answer, in the order illustrated below:

- **Listen to your audience**: Many of us think that communication is talking and, consequently, we tend to talk a lot. But good communication starts with listening. It is no surprise we have two ears and one mouth; listen twice and speak once. Respectfully listen to the entire question before responding to show attention and focus. Acknowledge the difference between *hearing* (accidental, effortless, and involuntary) and *listening* (focused, intentional, and voluntary).

- **Clarify or restate your question**: A good way to make sure you understand your customer's question, or simply to gain some precious seconds to think more about the question itself, is to repeat the question to your audience, asking for confirmation. Admit you are unsure about what your audience is asking, restate what your audience has just said, and ask for confirmation or examples. This approach will make your audience feel that you genuinely care about their question and you are striving to provide informational and accurate answers.

- **Strategize your answer**: When you phrase a response to your audience, keep in mind the following aspects:

154

○ <u>Be to the point</u>. Yes/No questions are often fine; you do not have to start re-inventing the wheel. Properly answer your question in an undisputable way and drill on demand. Ask your audience if they need to see or learn more; chances are that after you have "overwhelmed" your audience with many elaborate but thoughtful answers in the first 30 minutes of your presentation (see "first things first"), they will probably be okay with a Yes/No answer.

○ <u>Make it personal for your audience.</u> Use their terminology when answering a question; make it relevant for them so that they can follow you better and understand how your answer applies to their situation.

○ <u>Frame it to emphasize your competitor's weakness</u>. Without ever being aggressive or arrogant, indirectly call out your direct competitors by landing a few mines while presenting, using common expressions such as "other solutions out there" or "unlike other vendors in the industry." These sentences result in your audience taking notes and writing down what you know your competition will struggle with. Similarly, anticipate your competition by proactively telling your audience what your competition will most likely say about your company and your solution, and expose a valid mitigation strategy to that accusation.

○ <u>Address your audience by name</u>. Especially with remote meetings, this technique is extremely useful to bring the attention back to you as a presenter. Through the initial research you have done while preparing for this meeting, you know what the major pain points are for each of the attendees evaluating your product or solution. When it's time to show how your solution would make Susan's life easier, call her name openly by using sentences like, "*Susan, this is how we would handle your inventory reporting requirement,*" or *"This is something I believe you, John, would find useful; let me show you what I mean."*

o Use a whiteboard. Please do not stay put for a full hour behind a desk or a podium when presenting. Move around, engage with your audience, and make it dynamic. A winning technique in these regards is whiteboarding. A study from Corporate Visions has proven that whiteboard-style visuals outperform PowerPoint across some of the most critical areas of presentation impact, including recall, engagement, credibility, and perceptions of quality. Break up your standard demo flow by standing up, and draw up key aspects of your solution and how they impact your customer's needs. You do not need to be an artist for powerful visual storytelling; simply reach out to the whiteboard and make it memorable for your audience. Even ask your audience to approach the whiteboard and correct your rudimentary sketch by simply handing over the marker to them. What if you are delivering a presentation over the web? Most screen-sharing tools today offer white-boarding capabilities; if that is not the case, just bring up a blank slide or a blank Microsoft Excel sheet and use those basic tools as your virtual board. Whiteboarding is a very effective technique to engage with your audience and to make your message resonate with them.

- **Coordinate your answer**: Professionally-run meetings have one presenter speak at a time. Pre-agree with your team members on who answers what. As a trusted advisor, you should never take on any pricing question; that is something your salesperson should do. You should be focusing on your solution and your customer's business needs. Similarly, avoid piling up multiple answers. If a response has been provided already and your customer is satisfied with it, bypass the usual *"To add on to what Mary said."* There is no need to; your prospect is happy already, so move on and impress your audience with something else.

- **Show confidence**: Remember, you know your product and solution better than your audience does. From the moment you step in, to the moment you leave your meeting, your main goal is to inspire trust and credibility. The best way to do so is by showing confidence and conviction with any of the statements you discuss. Help yourself with non-verbal skills such as eye-contact or white-boarding techniques to establish your authority.

- **Confirm your answer**: It is always a best practice to ensure the answer you have just provided suitably addresses the question you have been asked. Sometimes, even after properly qualifying the question, maybe the answer is still not fully clear for your audience. At the end of your answer, simply double-check with your audience regarding the quality and meaningfulness of your answer; this will increase your credibility, show confidence, and also give you a chance to further articulate if your answer is not clear enough.

The Q&A Slide

Are you familiar with this slide?

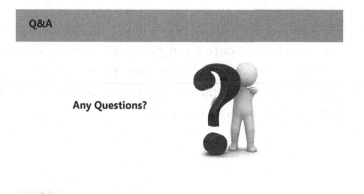

Figure 2.6.3. Standard Q&A Slide

I truly hope you are not, but I have a feeling you are. About 97% of sales presentations end up with a Q&A slide (53% of which show a question mark, 42% a raising hand, and the rest is left to the imagination) before the guaranteed "Thank You" slide.

Questions & Answers slides should not appear on any sales deck because:

- We are in the 21st century and have just taken digital selling to the extreme due to the recent global pandemic. If you truly are a Q&A aficionado, at least invite your audience to use the chat function of your screen-sharing device anytime during the presentation, not just at the end of the presentation.

- We run our presentations to be as interactive as possible; even if they are not, in cases of conference presentations with hundreds of users, we still do not need a Q&A slide. Why not? Read on.

- We are professional speakers; we use our mouth and words, we make ourselves heard loud and clear, and we control the room. In a nutshell, we *ask* if people have questions—we do not have them stare at a slide to remind them to think if they have any questions. We want to make it easier for them to ask questions without being forced. How? Read on.

- We want our last slide to be a summary of the main points we have touched on during our presentation and the value they bring to our customers. Having this information visible during the Q&A session at the end of the presentation will naturally help the audience ask questions.

Extra Tip!

There are many different ways to end a presentation that are mostly dependent on the style of the presenter. Besides summary slides, which I believe are the most effective as they are the ones to get the most photographs during a presentation, I have seen presenters end with a call-to-action slide, discussion starters, storytelling, or even with audience polls. The point here is this: if your presentation allows it, you should try to engage with your audience throughout your discussions. For those cases where it is not easy to do so for obvious formats or extended audiences, try to avoid those moments of awkwardness when people are asked if they have questions and no one dares to break the ice. Do not ask your audience for questions; enable your audience to spontaneously ask you questions.

Chapter 2.7 – Tips for Effective Demonstrations

This last chapter of "Excellence in Sales Engineering" provides a few useful tips to master this profession to perfection. Keeping the human aspect at the top of the list, we will start with a quick overview of what skills exceptional Sales Engineers must naturally possess or gradually develop. We will then explore how to leverage additional knowledgeable resources during the demo stage, provide a basic tool to guide us in our next demonstration, and wrap it up with a quick reminder of what Presales Engineers should and should not do.

Soft Skills in Presales

Knowing your solution or product inside out is of very little help if its values cannot be effectively communicated to your audience, making it genuinely interesting and engaging in your presentation.

One of the typical mistakes I see sales engineers running into is drilling in too many excruciating details of the solution they are describing, almost as if they were training their audience on how to use their products more than describing the benefits it would bring to them.

At other times, I see apathetic presenters simply aiming to go through their script without reading their audience, which in the meantime has lost complete trust and interest in the discussion. I've also run into sales engineers that know very little of what they are talking about, yet they sound astonishingly knowledgeable, educated, and are able to keep their customer's attention for prolonged amounts of time.

Keeping your audience engaged during a presentation, especially if spanning through multiple hours, requires mastering both verbal and non-verbal skills. We will see in a few moments what these skills are and how they can help you be a better Demo Guru. One quality often bypassed in many communication classes is what I refer to as the ability to understand the Room Temperature.

Reading the room is a vital skill any sales engineer should dominate.

It starts right when you step into the conference room or right when you hear your attendees introducing themselves during a remote web meeting. From the way they shake hands with you, make eye contact with you, or simply the tone of their introductions via the phone, you should be able to gauge whether it will be a monolithic or active audience; therefore, you should plan to behave accordingly. Better yet, during an onsite presentation, pay attention to the way your customer's team members take their seats, focusing on who sits next to whom and intercepting the looks team members share during the presentation. This is a good indicator to determine how good or bad you are doing. First impressions might not always be right, but they should not be underestimated.

The ability to read people's moods and engagement styles is certainly a huge help with any demonstration but will not do the job if your verbal and non-verbal skills are not up to par.

True Story: The Terrifying CEO

I was once on a sales call where I was presenting to an evaluation committee of around a dozen members for a medium- to small-sized organization in the New England area. When I first saw the committee coming down the aisle from the floor-to-ceiling glass doors of the conference room I was seated in, I already got an idea of the type of situation I was about to find myself in. An assertive woman, the CEO of the prospect's US Division, fully absorbed in her phone, was walking relentlessly towards me with, right behind her, an army of 10+ men and women silently following her lead. When they made it to the room, the CEO shook my hand and my salesperson's hand and told us right away she wanted everybody to sit first. So we did. Interestingly enough, the CEO's direct reports were sitting in front of the CEO with more junior analysts sitting next to her. For the first 45 minutes, the presentation was mostly a two-person conversation, where the customers' team members were communicating among each other by writing down their notes on a piece of paper, folding it so that the only readable information would be the name of the addressee, and passing it around. The only person asking the question was the CEO, based on the folded papers that made their way to her. Completely against my nature, I became part of the status quo and adapted to the process without blinking. When the CEO left the room for another meeting, followed by the analyst sitting to her left, a member of the selection team apologized for the "heavy atmosphere," saying their CEO does not like "chaotic situations" with a hint of sarcasm. Picking up on that sarcasm was the key to the meeting. By sincerely respecting the situation but respectfully defusing it, I was able to connect with the rest of the team for the remainder of the presentation who, in turn, appeared to be a very friendly, open, and cooperative audience.

In the following pages, we will examine some key skills in both verbal communication and body language, reminding ourselves of Professor Albert Mehrabian's Rule of Personal Communication:

Elements of Communication

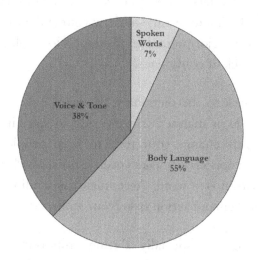
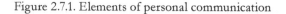

Figure 2.7.1. Elements of personal communication

Verbal Skills

Choosing the appropriate words is fundamental to making sure the audience we are interacting with properly understands, elaborates, and retains the message we want to communicate to them. This is particularly true when we have to hit on key positioning items. Our marketing teams spend many hours crafting the most innovative messaging process for our solutions that we owe it to them to properly relay it to the public. However, words are not enough. They have to be communicated, and the way we organize and speak our words depends on many collateral factors that go well beyond the actual terms we use.

- Pace: The Merriam-Webster dictionary defines "pace" as the "rate of performance or delivery." In simpler terms, pace commonly refers to how fast you talk. Increase your pace when you want to create enthusiasm and excitement and slow down when you want to make a point and require attention.

- Volume: No dictionary references needed for this; volume commonly refers to how loud you speak. Soften your voice for a limited amount of time to draw your audience in and raise it to make a major point. Never adopt a low volume that would show a lack of confidence.

- Tone: Back to the dictionary, Merriam-Webster defines tone as a "style or manner of expression in speaking or writing." Constantly change your tone to keep people engaged and convey emotions or make specific points by breaking up the tone within one word. Accentuate the ending syllables of a word to demand action from your audience.

- Articulation: Especially during important presentations, spontaneous memory loss (SML) could play a tricky factor in the way you pronounce your words. Articulate all words properly, especially on the phone, and avoid swallowing any word. Practice any term that is particularly challenging for you by repeating it aloud many times before your presentation.

Many other considerations apply to verbal skills—avoid filler words, speak with confidence, be clear and on point, do not talk too much for too long, etc.—but the ones listed above are usually the hardest to govern. The key to mastering verbal skills is to learn how to control yourself; constant practice is what will allow you to harmonize pace, tone, volume, and articulation, making your speech sound natural and captivating.

Non-Verbal Skills

The rule of Personal Communication: 7-38-55. The biggest contributing factor to effective communication is non-verbal skills, namely your body language. Poker players are the best example in this respect—they use minimal words and focus on their body language. Without taking it to the extreme, if a colleague of yours says "I don't have a problem with you" while avoiding eye-contact, with arms crossed at their chest, and in a nervous tone, probably you, as the listener, will not fully believe your colleague. You are, instead, encouraged to trust the most predominant form of communication: non-verbal communication. Pay close attention to the following when demonstrating software:

- <u>Posture:</u> Keep your upper body erect but not rigid. Lean forward when listening to a question to show interest and lean backward when responding to show confidence.

- <u>Eye Contact:</u> Look into the eyes of all of your attendees at least once and maintain at least five seconds of contact with each listener. Keep going back to the decision maker in the room to make constant eye-contact.

- <u>Movement:</u> Movement captivates the eye and ignites attention. Stand up and move purposefully towards your destination with no back and forth.

- <u>Gestures:</u> Combine movements with gestures and voice tone to show energy and enthusiasm and to emphasize important points for the audience. Control hand gestures to draw attention to what you want them to focus on.

- <u>Facial Expressions:</u> Accentuate smiling to transmit happiness and pride, wink in appropriate circumstances to boost your listener's ego and increase complicity, and open your eyes wide to show interest.

- <u>Left and Right:</u> Move to the left when you openly highlight some negatives of a competitor's solution or offering and to the right to relay positive content about your company and product. Keep it consistent: associate negatives with your left and positives with your right a few more times to deliver good news or bad news. Next time you want your audience to perceive a certain topic as negative without you openly stating so, go to the left: your audience's brains will naturally assign bad feelings towards that topic.

- <u>Smile:</u> Smiling is contagious and naturally brings down barriers. Genuine smiles, where even your eyes "smile," have scientifically proven to create a sense of comradeship and usually set the right tone for the rest of the presentation.

The main goal of properly leveraging your body language is to create empathy and solidify your perception as a trusted advisor. Simply restating a script that scores on all the right points but lacks enthusiasm, passion, energy, and connection with your audience will not do the job. Remember: people buy from people.

| MAXIMIZING NON-VERBAL COMMUNICATION ||
Tip	How & Why
Strategize the start	Practice your intro lines to convey energy and passion by writing a few words down
Accentuate your accent	Whether a regional or a foreign accent, people will notice it, so play with it
Know your emotions	Transform anxiety and tension into fight-mode adrenaline
Stay focused	In case of questions that cannot be answered, avoid coughing, nervously swallowing, or using filler words

Table 2.7.1. Tips for Maximizing Non-verbal Communication Skills

 **Recommendation:**

After more than a decade of giving presentations, the adrenaline is always high and the willingness to do extraordinarily well is always there, just like on day one. Here are some routines I follow to excel at any presentation I am involved with. While personal, my blunt recommendation is to try to

assess and criticize yourself; your co-workers might be too busy to sit on your presentations and provide feedback or maybe are just too nice to give you constructive criticism. The best judge of your work, in this case, is yourself; record your web presentation and watch it twice. First without audio to focus on gestures, movements, and overall engagement. Then, turn the audio on the second time and focus on filler words, tone, volume, and articulation.

Involving Your Professional Services Team in Demos

It is a team effort, after all. Strategic deals are not simply a one-person job; they are rather the result of a cohesive team that acts like a task force trying to gain that business. Marketing will help direct us to the most adequate collaterals or maybe even draft new ones just for the occasion. Channel will support us by giving us access to certified partners willing to team up with us. Finance will be ready to deviate from our margin targets to simply acquire the business, and even our top management has made itself available for executive sponsorship.

In this perfect storm, Professional Services, the consulting leg of your organization that will help your prospect install, implement, and get the most of the solution you are demoing, plays a vital role.

Professional Services brings reality and adds substance to the conversation with real-life use cases in a way that people not directly involved cannot do. Not all consultants have the adequate skillset to be involved in a sales cycle. Given their background and expertise, junior consultants tend to focus more on the problem than the solution, making it look cumbersome for a prospective client to adopt our solution.

More seasoned consultants that have experienced and successfully managed multiple challenges could instead open up the prospect's eyes to a variety of different solutions. No matter your experience in a specific topic, when you need to show deep knowledge and accomplished expertise, you must tap into your consulting pool and have them join your meeting. The most effective format during the presentation is that of a natural conversation between you, the presenter, and your Professional Services people. Of course, you will be doing most of the talking—articulating your customer's needs into a product demonstration—but here and there, expect your coworker from Professional Services to jump in with best practices, statistics, common fallbacks, and mitigation strategies from a customer he or she was visiting just the day before. Having your Professional Services Team participate in key strategic demonstrations adds credibility and trustworthiness to your sales cycle, giving your prospective customers a chance to fully appreciate the experience and knowledge they will be receiving by doing business with you.

If used wisely and methodically, Professional Services' involvement in the sales cycle is priceless.

True Story: Never Be Afraid to Ask for Help!

Probably one of the best intuitions I have ever had. I picked up the phone and my sales rep delivered the great news: we had been shortlisted for a huge Financial Services Organization we had worked so hard on, and they wanted us on site the following week to present to the entire team, roughly 30 people. I had always been told banks speak their own language, so I decided to bring my top Financial Services specialist with me to the demo. Boy, was that a smart move! Thirty minutes into the demonstration, my coworker and I were alternating product demonstration with best practices, sharing real-life stories from a customer down the street, and were even gaining credibility by stating how cool the feature I was showing was but how little it's used in reality. Pairing yourself as a presenter with a subject guru adding color and substance to your statements fosters credibility and increases your chance of winning the deal.

Dos and Don'ts in Presales

We have provided many suggestions already as we were analyzing the many areas with which Demo Gurus are involved. In this chapter, we will briefly recap what to focus on and what to avoid across the main steps of the sales cycles, with the intent to provide a quick reference for all sales engineers, depending on what step of the sales cycle they are called to help on.

As usual, though, first things first! Too many times, we focus on improving or nurturing niche skills that will undoubtedly make a difference during a presentation, forgetting, however, about the basics. Following is a quick reminder for all of us:

- Mouse Control. Avoid motion sickness. Your mouse is a pointer and should be used to point to the areas you want to reach in your software demonstration. Watching a cursor zipping around on the screen aimlessly or, even worse, spinning in circles to highlight a keyword or menu, could be very distracting to the audience. Simply click only on what you want to explain and pause until your next click; do not move the mouse around and do not touch it to avoid unnecessary flickering or annoying cursor shakes. When scrolling up and down, assume your audience is interested in reading what you are browsing through on your page; don't scroll down too fast to avoid overwhelming your attendees.

- You are not a trainer. Your job is not to train your audience on how to use your product; your job is to have them understand the benefits they will achieve by using your solution. This approach inherently implies staying away from explaining in detail how the most hidden features and functions of your offerings work. Focus instead on the value they will bring to your audience and how other existing customers are using and benefitting from them. This does not mean you should not be an expert with your product; it rather means using that knowledge appropriately, at the right time, and for the right audience. Remember to "drill on demand."

- <u>Keep an eye on time.</u> Avoid running out of time. Staying within your allotted time increases your audience's perception of you as a professional presenter that is respectful of their time. Running out of time shows you are not in control of your meeting and makes the solution you are offering seem complex. Don't make the rookie mistake of packing as much content as your time slot permits. Allow for interaction, questions, and side discussions, and plan on finishing at least 5 or 10 minutes before your time is up. Remember your sidekick; your salesperson is there to help you stay on track and on time!

- <u>Prepare, Research, and Practice</u>. This is an obvious statement that requires no explanation other than a reminder from Benjamin Franklin who once said, "By failing to prepare, you are preparing to fail."

- <u>Do not beat a dead horse</u>. Sometimes software crashes. It's normal, and it's part of the game. No matter how good your QA team is, or how many times you have tried those clicks before, the system might crash during a demo. If it happens, do not panic! And do not attempt to give it another try; chances are that you will get the same error, and it will draw your audience's attention to the crash you are experiencing. Similarly, avoid statements like "I have never seen this error," or "This has never happened to me before." These words convey an unstable and unreliable solution. If you can, quickly get rid of the error message on your screen and move on with your presentation without creating a harsh separation from the point you wanted to prove when the crash happened and your next topic. In case the crash is not a simple malfunction but an impediment to continue, ask for a few minutes while you try to fix the error.

Disconnect from any projector or screen sharing tool or ask your sales partner to jump in and take your time to investigate your issue. Bear in mind the old saying "try turning it off and on again" sometimes does the trick. If not, don't forget to notify that error to your Product Development team!

Now that we have our basics down, let's take this discussion to the next level, and let's examine the Do's and Don'ts sales engineers should pay attention to throughout the sales cycle.

Dos	Don'ts
Listen, understand, and learn	Simply take notes
Demonstrate industry-related experience	Focus on today's challenges
Drive questions with storytelling	Ask too many questions
Uncover problems	Overpromise
Build the relationship and trust	Be "selly"
	Focus on the product ONLY

Table 2.7.2. Dos and Don'ts during the Discovery Phase

Dos	Don'ts
Translate discovery call into requirements (know their story)	Assume a standard demo is enough
Align strategy with Sales and other departments if necessary	Skip the research
Understand the IT landscape	Take the competition or audience for granted

Evaluate partner/executive involvement	Overcomplicate the topics/agenda
Know your competition and the sales cycle	Focus on the product ONLY
Learn about your audience and Champions	
Incorporate the cheesy customizations	
Share the agenda and meeting goals	

Table 2.7.3. Dos and Don'ts during the Pre-demo Phase

Dos	Don'ts
Bring passion and eagerness	Stick to the demo flow no matter what
Set the stage and confirm agenda/attendees	Get lost in the weeds
Tackle the "easy stuff" first	Feel like you HAVE TO use all the allocated time
Build your reputation right away (questions, case studies, etc.)	Speak for the entire meeting
Read and react to your audience	Train your audience
Raise the bar	Be afraid to park questions
Solidify reputation as the SME	Focus on the product ONLY
Open the prospects' eyes	

Table 2.7.4. Dos and Don'ts during the Intro-demo Phase

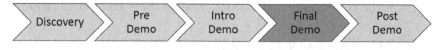

Dos	Don'ts
Stay focused/control the scope	Assume everyone has seen the product
Map "proof-points" to the agenda	Assume everyone *remembers* seeing the product
Differentiate	Simply replicate an existing process
Tailor the meeting for your audience	Wait until the last 10 minutes to deliver the "wow effect"
Involve Professional Services	Focus on the product ONLY
Prove your worth	
Involve the prospect	
Make it unique to remember	

Table 2.7.5. Dos and Don'ts during the Final-demo Phase

Dos	Don'ts
Address any parked questions	Use generic leave-behinds
Address anything unclear/ misinformation	Forget the services hand-off
Send screenshots of "wow-factors"	Forget to follow up
Send digital assets (case studies, videos, full demos)	Focus on the product ONLY
Ask for Executive briefing (summary of benefits and differentiators)	
Coordinate with marketing and sales for leave-behinds and reference calls	

Table 2.7.6. Dos and Don'ts during the Post-demo Phase

What is the common denominator across all these recommendations?

DO NOT FOCUS ON THE PRODUCT ONLY.

The product or solution you are demoing is meant to provide value and benefits for your prospects. As we said a few times now, look at your offering as a launching pad to help your audience understand the scary reality of sticking with their current solution and process, and open their eyes to the tremendous possibilities they could explore by adopting your product. Use your solution's features and functions to support value selling.

Demo Preparedness Checklist

As a Demo Guru responsible for the North American Presales department of an international organization, I had to make my life easier.

Having to keep an eye on my team members across different locations and coach them on how to best tackle the opportunity they were working on, I came up with a Demo Preparedness Checklist that all my team members still refer to when they've been assigned an opportunity. This checklist is also automated in our CRM solution, making it easier for me to jump in and guide my peers towards success.

In its most concise form, the checklist divides the demo cycle into multiple phases:

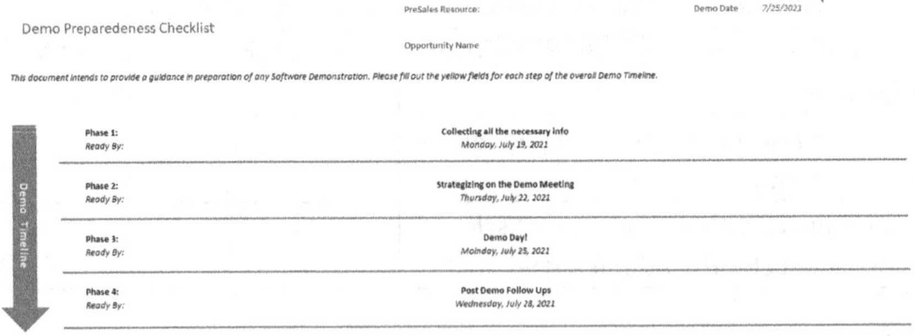
Demo Preparedeness Checklist

PreSales Resource:

Demo Date 7/25/2021

Opportunity Name

This document intends to provide a guidance in preparation of any Software Demonstration. Please fill out the yellow fields for each step of the overall Demo Timeline.

Demo Timeline

Phase 1: *Ready By:*	**Collecting all the necessary info** *Monday, July 19, 2021*
Phase 2: *Ready By:*	**Strategizing on the Demo Meeting** *Thursday, July 22, 2021*
Phase 3: *Ready By:*	**Demo Day!** *Moinday, July 25, 2021*
Phase 4: *Ready By:*	**Post Demo Follow Ups** *Wednesday, July 28, 2021*

Figure 2.7.2. A condensed View of the Demo Preparedness Checklist

By specifying a demo date, a simple calculation will establish due dates of when each phase should be completed. Leveraging more automated and robust solutions, the due date of each activity will translate into a task assigned to the sales engineer, who will receive a task reminder right on his or her calendar.

Each demo phase is then divided into a series of actions that aim to double-check we are setting ourselves up for success for that specific touchpoint, and if not, take action.

Phase 1 is about collecting all the information we need before our demo; this does not imply that we should look for this information ourselves, as some of it should come from our salesperson's qualification of the deal. What this means is that, one way or another, we need this information to be effective on our demo day.

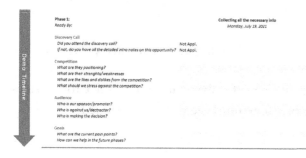

Figure 2.7.3. Detailed Steps of Phase 1 of the Demo Preparedness Checklist

Phase 2 refers to the strategy we want to follow during the presentation now that we have collected and digested all of the information from the prior step. The goal of this phase is to catch up with the salesperson and decide on the best strategy for the meeting.

Figure 2.7.4. Detailed Steps of Phase 2 of the Demo Preparedness Checklist

Phase 3 is all about your Demo Day! The list of tasks in this phase aims to remind sales engineers of some basics that we all tend to forget, especially when it comes to demo equipment and audience.

Figure 2.7.5. Detailed Steps of Phase 3 of the Demo Preparedness Checklist

Phase 4 is all about post-demo feedback and a reminder for us sales engineers that we are not done until the contract is signed!

Figure 2.7.6. Detailed Steps of Phase 4 of the Demo Preparedness Checklist

This checklist is by no means exhaustive, nor should it aim to micromanage any experienced sales engineer. It should only serve as a modus-operandi and a thought-process schema for any presales professional to provide value throughout any step of the sales cycle.

Extra Tip!

The checklist above shows how connected the professional life of a Sales Engineer is with that of a Sales Account Executive. It is in the interest of both parties that the relationship you have as a Demo Guru with your assigned AE is as transparent and open as possible. Do invest time in evolving and cultivating that relationship so you both come to leverage each other's strengths and contain and correct each other's weaknesses. There is no hurting anybody's feelings when negative feedback is provided critically and factually with the sole intent of improving. Be open to feedback and make sure you provide feedback to your AE.

The Pyramid of Habits

Following best practices, here is a quick recap of everything we have discussed so far in this section.

Figure 2.7.7. Habits of Excellent Demo Gurus

I have purposely selected the image of a pyramid to remind you of the three main habits we need to embrace as excellent Demo Gurus. Stuck in between symbolism and practicality, I have always asked myself what the most important layer of Egyptian Pyramids might be.

Is it the base holding the entire structure?

Or, is it rather the apex allowing the structure itself to reach its goal?

Or, is it the middle-layer linking the base to the apex?

If pyramids were built that way more than 4,000 years ago and are still standing today, it is fair to assume all layers have a purpose and work perfectly together.

Fast forward to the era of enterprise software; the Pyramid of Habits for excellent Demo Gurus also has three layers, and the order of importance is still a mystery, at least to me.

- Sales Alignment. Sales Reps and Sales Engineers share the same mission: close the sale. Both sides of the team have to be able to work smoothly together, complete each other's sentences, understand when the counterpart needs help, and strategize together on what is best for the customer to be more effective and win the deal. I suggest all Demo Gurus and all Sales Reps welcome constructive criticism: be open and honest with each other. Only by having a direct line of communication, at the risk of appearing to step on each other's toes, will it be possible to effectively gain improvement and aim for excellence.

- Preparation. No demo is like any prior, and every prospective customer is different. Not necessarily in the way they conduct business or their needs. On the contrary, each prospective client approaches the buying process uniquely and translates what they see into what they need in their own way. Only through thorough research and preparation will you be able to connect with your audience. Do not underestimate the power of prep-work, and remember, there is no such thing as a "standard demo." Each demo should be tailored to the audience you will meet. By researching your prospect's DNA, you will be able to craft valuable content in the form of an enjoyable demo flow.

- Passion. People buy from people. People have emotions and expect empathy. It's a primary psychological need for people to know others and understand their situation. There is no repeatable playbook in Enterprise Software Sales that one can follow word by word and be successful. There is instead the expectation that sales presales consultants are credible, passionate, and inspiring human beings willing to educate others. Humanize the sale transaction by showing dedication, enthusiasm, and excitement in every step of the buying process.

Chapter 2.8 – The Demo Guru Dilemma

As Demo Gurus, we love our products, and we are naturally eager to show how great our solution is. We take pride in investing an excruciating amount of time replicating our customer's current issues to show how their lives can improve with our approach. The best of us try to prepare for every question we might get asked during a demonstration, maybe even spending long nights to make sure our custom demo assets look impeccable.

However, how much is enough? When should we pull the trigger and stop "over preparing"? How do we know when we are ready to go?

Every human being reacts differently to emotions, including stress and trepidation. It is almost impossible to suggest when the right time is for you, the Demo Guru, to turn off your computer and get some sleep.

In the following pages, we will highlight a simple procedural framework to help Sales Engineers show up at Demo Day with their clearest minds as well as achieve and sustain a healthy work-life balance.

The CLEAR framework

Being the first one in the office and the last one to leave your desk is not synonymous with being a hard-worker.

While I do believe that specific circumstances might require extra effort and longer hours every once in a while, it is not the intention of your CEO to have you work day and night to meet a deadline. Your direct manager will have a key role in assessing your ability to execute and plan your workload accordingly, but most of your workload realistically depends on yourself.

With that "entrepreneurial" mindset that characterizes stellar Demo Gurus, it is fundamental you proactively manage your time to optimize your outputs and get to your Demo Day in your best shape.

The recommendations below should help you take ownership of your schedule and increase your performance on the job while contributing to a better work-life balance:

C – Calendarize your workweek

L – Leave your phone behind

E – Estimate efforts and workloads

A – Assess risks

R – Reach out for help

Let's now take a deeper look at what these suggestions specifically entail:

- Calendarizing your week is extremely important and immensely helpful to ensure you are not dragged into meetings you should not be part of. Blocking some time on your work calendar will allow you to focus on your task at hand. This does not mean it's necessary to make yourself unavailable to your co-workers eight hours a day; it simply means dedicating specific slots of your workday to yourself and others. Typically, it is wise to leave the early morning calendar slots and the early afternoon open for team stand up calls or check-in calls with your colleagues. The central parts of your mornings and the central part of your afternoons instead should appear as "Busy" to any of your teammates trying to schedule a call with you, allowing you to focus on your activities while not losing track of what the rest of the team is working on for the same account.

- Leave your phone behind, especially during those "busy" time slots you have reserved for yourself on the calendar. Not being in a meeting with somebody else does not mean you are available to take on sudden phone calls or check your emails constantly. Pretend instead that you are in the middle of a demonstration. You would not check emails while in front of a prospective customer. Instead, you are laser-focused on what your audience is asking. The "busy" time on your calendar is nothing different; you have those dedicated slot to work for your prospective customers, and you should solely be focused on them.

- Estimating the amount of effort your task will require is fundamental to properly manage your workload, especially if you are an experienced Sales Engineer with adequate knowledge of both the industry you operate in and the product you demonstrate. Do not commit to what you won't be able to deliver. This does not mean deliberately under committing—it is all about objectively quantifying the amount of work required to complete the task assigned to you so you can inform your sales counterpart and he/she can schedule the next demonstration in line with your indications.

- **A**ssess Your Risks. Every plan has risks and opportunities and every plan, especially when a deadline is set with an external audience, should have some sort of backup plan in the case of impediments to the original plan. Identifying the risks and communicating the perceived risks with the larger team creates a sense of accountability for the entire team, who is now aware of the potential drawbacks and will be more inclined to lend a helping hand. As I always used to say to my team, "Let me know when you smell smoke before you see fire."

- **R**each out for help. In other words, there is no need to be a hero. If you have gained a reputation as a hard-worker and high-performer with good ethical behaviors within your organization, both your manager and your peers will be willing to help. It might be in the form of technical assistance from other members of the organization or maybe educational support for topics with which you are not too familiar. Raising your hand and asking for help is never a sign a vulnerability or deficiency. Conversely, if properly articulated, it builds up your credibility as it shows how much you want that sales opportunity to turn into a success.

The goal of the CLEAR approach is not to tell the Sales Engineer when enough is enough. Its objective is to set up a behavioral approach so that Demo Gurus can get to their Demo Day with a CLEAR mindset.

 **Recommendation:**

I am a true believer that what makes a difference in any meeting is a clear mindset that allows people to focus and intelligently think on their feet when any question is asked. Even today, before any important meeting and especially during my presales days, I block off my calendar 15 minutes before showtime. This allows me to quietly go through my extra checks, but more importantly, it is time for me to decompress, complete any kind of adjustment

I want to make to my presentation assets, and clear my mind. Even if your demo assets are not fully completed, try to give yourself some time before the start of your meeting so you can gather your thoughts. I can guarantee you that a healthy and sharp mindset is far better and undoubtedly more important than not having all your demo examples fully baked. Take this time instead to close all your computer windows, get ready with your first demo screen, and grab some coffee while reading the latest news!

 **Extra Tip!**

The term "email pollution" refers to the ever-increasing load of messages you receive daily in your inbox. As an exercise, during any given week, keep a note of the actual emails you have received and keep track of those that you have received just for informational purposes. Also, keep track of those you received as the main recipient, those you received as part of a distribution list, and those you have received from external newsletters you probably subscribed to many moons ago. You will soon realize that the majority of emails that land in your inbox is of no interest to you. Actually, they are a distraction. If you cannot resist the temptation of flipping on your phone to look at the sender, use the advanced feature on your phone that allows you to assign dedicated ringtones or special illumination to those people in your organization from whom you do not want to miss an email. Your phone will probably ring less than five times a day!

PART 3: EMBRACING SALES ENGINEERING

Chapter 3.1 – Presales Beyond Demos

In the very first pages of this book, we explained what Demo Gurus do and do not do. One of the statements in that paragraph says that Sales Engineers do not simply do demos, but, using a similar illustration already presented, they should contribute to many other areas of the organization.

We have already extensively covered how presales contributes to the sales cycle. The rest of the upcoming pages will, therefore, focus on how Sales Engineers can help many other departments beyond the sales organization.

Let's analyze them one by one:

Figure 3.1.1. Presales Areas of Intervention

Product Management: This term refers to the most important function of any corporation selling a product. Product Management is the hub of the entire lifecycle of a product: from its idealization and development to commercialization and support—with historically a natural focus on the development component. Sales engineers can significantly help the Product Management team by influencing their core activity: the development of the product or solution they will be demoing. Presales should, in theory, be the best advocate to influence the product direction and roadmap together with the end customers. By being constantly in the field and directly in touch with the prospect's requests and challenges, the presales team must communicate with the product management team to propose product enhancements to help shape the future roadmap. Also, presales probably has the best knowledge of the competition, being exposed to them in their demonstrations, giving them an advantage in coordinating with the product management team to study the competitor's offering and

189

enhance the solution. As a professional sales engineer, make your voice heard within the product management organization of your company. Attend official product roadmap refinery meetings, sprint reviews, release planning sessions, or any other formal gatherings to learn about any new functionality, and voice your concerns or express your suggestions for the future direction of the solution you will be demoing. Remember, it is in your best interest to actively participate in the improvement of your company's products; you will be the first user of those products during a very delicate situation—demoing to a prospective buyer.

PR & Communications: Sales engineers' natural background of technical knowledge and sales skills makes the presales department the perfect candidate for promoting the solution both internally and externally. Demo Gurus are the best resources to translate even the most complicated technical details into tangible value for the non-technical audience. As subject matter experts, presales professionals should be constantly evangelizing the company and solutions they represent, beyond the day of the demo itself. Blogging about specific market or technology trends and producing whitepapers, podcasts, or videos on relevant topics are all routine activities that should be part of any presales professionals' work-load. This approach has several obvious advantages: it helps brand awareness and brings the company's solution to the forefront of prospects' minds compared to other products/services in the market, and it builds trust and confidence that presenters need to inspire with their speech. There are multiple moments when presales should jump in to help with communication and evangelization efforts. Think of any major product release announcements; presales should be contributing to the new launch with press releases, blogs, and public webcasts to show the new features being released. Future developments the product team is undertaking should also represent a good source of evangelization. Generating interest about something that will launch at a later date creates suspense and expectations in the market. Presales could also constantly promote their solutions to educate their customer base and increase revenue from contract renewals or cross-selling opportunities. Sales engineers possess the right talent to intrigue existing customers to adopt new features or products, expanding the use of the solution and increasing the Annual Recurring Revenue (ARR).

Marketing: There are many definitions of the word "marketing" and it would be unfair to pick one versus the other. One thing is sure, though; especially in the world of SaaS solutions, the Marketing Department has increased its relevance and has one of the most challenging responsibilities within a company. SaaS solutions that are little known in the market they operate in struggle three times more, on average, to sell their solutions than more well-known and better-penetrated organizations even with less valid products. As Investopedia put it, "the ultimate goal of a marketing function is to match a company's products and services to the people who need and want them." Presales, once again, is a perfect candidate to help in this area: sales engineers' backgrounds can support the marketing team in identifying the best target for the solutions they are intimately familiar with, develop the most appropriate messaging to attract that audience, and deliver on the promotion of the company's products and services. Seasoned sales engineers should expect their marketing department to involve them in defining any marketing strategy they are interested in pursuing: from the initial idealization of market/audience, to addressing the pains and needs the campaign should focus on, to the final evangelization. Too many times, presales is only involved at the end of the process in the form of presenting at a conference, hosting a webinar, or co-presenting at a luncheon that marketing has set up independently. When this happens, presales is not bringing the value it could potentially contribute had they been involved in the actual creation of that marketing initiative.

Product Marketing: This is absolutely a non-negotiable area where presales needs to be involved at all costs. With the expression "Product Marketing," we are typically referring to the process of defining the detailed positioning and value proposition of a specific offering. Product Marketing is usually a function of the overall Marketing Department but, while the latter is focused on the overall strategy to penetrate and attract a specific audience, Product Marketing teams are more often focused on helping the actual sale. In other words, even if Product Marketing generally reports to marketing, their efforts are most frequently appreciated by the sales teams as they are the producers of all those nice collaterals such as brochures, infographics, or even presentation decks that our salespeople leverage to close their deals. It is rare to find product marketers that have deep product knowledge, even if that will be the preferred profile; this is when a sales engineer can help tremendously. Presales should be working very closely with the Product Marketing teams to make sure the assets they produce are effective enough and should stay away from generic messaging at all costs. With their deep product expertise, industry experience, and competitive knowledge, Demo Gurus should team up with the Product Marketing organization to put substance and relevance to the messaging and positioning of the datasheets, brochures, flyers, and decks they produce. Product Marketing possesses the right knowledge for identifying the best means of communication to help the sales departments sell faster and close more deals, but not too often do they possess the proper knowledge to effectively communicate product differentiators or adequately address the most hidden and pressing needs the customers might have. The utmost testimonial to a fruitful collaboration between the Product Marketing team and the Presales organization is a corporate deck that salespeople can talk to and do not find it too "selly" themselves!

Enablement: I have never truly believed in the saying from Francis Bacon that "Knowledge is power." However, I am a full believer that the real power comes by sharing the knowledge you have. The strength of an organization comes from what its people know, how efficiently they use what they know, and how open and fast they are to acquire new knowledge. Even the best products and solutions on the market do not simply sell themselves. At some point in time, someone very intimate with those products and services shared his or her knowledge and made it public with other individuals that, in turn, did just the same. Presales learn valuable information on the product or solutions they demonstrate—their positioning, their differentiators, their strengths, and their weaknesses; it is therefore logical for them to share that knowledge with the rest of the organization. Fear not, sales engineers should not be kept accountable for sales enablement! The most structured and efficient organizations typically have a Sales Operations team that supports the sales force by providing them with all the guidance they need. The way presales should enable sales, or any other department within the organization, is by providing that extra layer of reality and experience from the fields they own. Sales engineers should help run internal workshops to discuss positioning, messaging, effective competition handling, and, most importantly, highlight what their customers are constantly asking and how their solutions can address those demands.

Channel: With this term, we are referring to the potential network of partners that an organization relies on to promote and implement its products and services. To effectively leverage and optimize the channel network—at least at the beginning when external resellers are learning about your offering—it is crucial to see and treat the partner force as a pure extension of the main team. Therefore, anything that has been discussed so far applies to the Channel organization, as well. The only difference when it comes to the partner function, which is not a different need per se than other internal functions, is the constant struggle to ensure they are representing your company and solutions properly. It is widely agreed that this should be a problem of the Alliance Manager or the specific position dedicated to managing and growing the partner network. It should also be agreed upon, however, that for delicate situations such as product demonstrations where, oddly enough, the deal is either lost or won in most of the circumstances during the demo itself, the sales engineering organization can help ensure the partner network does proper justice to the products they are promoting independently. Presales, therefore, should be involved in sessions with the partner network to talk details and assist with partner-led demos, especially considering those same partners might be representing other competitive solutions. This requires deep product knowledge to face any specific question that might come up, deep knowledge of the competition to effectively differentiate, and a clear understanding of the business requirements that might be brought up—simple tasks for any seasoned sales engineer.

 **Recommendation:**

I have been running a Presales organization for a few years. One of the main points I always used to make when I was interviewing new candidates was to clarify that what they were applying for was not the typical demo job where they would be giving two or three demos a day following a predefined script. I always made sure, instead, that any candidate would be able and willing to embark on many areas where their knowledge and hard work could be appreciated by the organization. Maybe just out of luck, I have been able to build a team of presales professionals who not only look at their demos as a necessary step in the overall buying cycle but have fully embraced helping their organization from a marketing, channel, sales, and product development perspective. My team collaborates closely with the product marketing department for digital initiatives that aim to show the key features of our application. They contribute to product management by constantly submitting product enhancements based on their experience in the fields. And they also help with training and enablement activities across many areas of the organization, from new sales hires onboarding to partner training. What is in it for them? Why should a sales engineer prefer being involved in so many activities rather than following a safe script every day to deliver a winning canned demo? Personality plays a huge role, and being exposed to so many areas of the organization that drive the business significantly benefits you as a sales engineer. On one side, you could be part of the actual strategy of your organization and effectively gain experience in areas that could come in handy in the future. On the other, exposing yourself to so many different aspects of the company will give you extended visibility. It is on you to get out of your comfort zone and play your cards well!

 **Extra Tip!**

There are not many other roles in an organization that have the luxury of being exposed to so many different functions like the Presales role does. With a mindset focused on future career growth, Sales Engineers should be active contributors in many of the departments mentioned above. This allows them to test their appetite for a potential future lateral move while being noticed by other members of the organization.

Chapter 3.2 – Working with Your Sales Reps

It is a common thought that has crossed every sales engineer's mind multiple times in their career: How do sales reps keep themselves busy eight hours a day? Reality is that being a quota carrier, like any sales executive, is not an easy job.

There is a lot of stress in trying to reach a sales target that was committed in the latest forecast call, and there are certainly many touchpoints with prospective customers to follow up on with which often presales is not involved.

Think of when you, as a sales engineer, get brought into the opportunity. Most likely, your sales counterpart has spent numerous hours pitching your company and your solution, has mapped out all the relevant players to address before and during the demo, and has built the right rapport of trust and respect with the key decision makers. Not to mention the insane number of hours salespeople spend cold calling or researching a way to get in front of a customer and the necessary administrative tasks that their job implies, like Opportunity Plans, Close Plans, Territory Account Plans, Quarterly Business Reviews (QBRs), etc.

And the post-demo work is not something to be underestimated, either. From additional follow-ups, to further value selling and positioning, all the way through negotiation and contract redlining, sales executives spend a lot more than just the two hours of demo time we spend with them on Demo Day. To top it all off, forecasting and reporting to their sales managers can be intensive and time-consuming tasks, especially in bigger organizations.

What all of this means is that selling is not easy. Even the most "corporate" salespeople have to fight against a common perception of mistrust and sometimes dishonesty that makes all future customer interactions harder to begin with. Customers can be unfair in some cases and ask for the moon when in reality they have already made up their minds. Not to mention the competition in today's commoditization of many products and solutions makes the sale and the related margin not easy to dominate and excel at.

The rule of the game when it comes to Presales working with Sales is PARTNERSHIP.

Some might believe that presales is just in charge of the "technical sale" while the "business sale" is in charge of the salesperson. When such a dichotomy exists, sales and presales tend to experience friction with each other resulting in the following unproductive criticism:

SALES CRITICISM OF PRESALES	PRESALES CRITICISM OF SALES
Too technical	Poor deal qualification
Too training oriented	Poor control of deal cycle
Talks too much without breaks	Poor meeting preparation
Too much information	Poor expectation management
Does not adjust to customer's needs and only sticks to the generic demo flow	Does not know what the product can / cannot do and interrupts with incorrect statements.

I personally do not agree with differentiating a sale between its technical and commercial aspects; there is only one type of sale translating into a final order.

Thinking presales has completed its job just because the demo went extraordinarily well is selfish and just foolish.

Thinking that a sales cycle is all about the product demonstration is also selfish and foolish.

Presales has the responsibility of converting any potential opportunity into a sales booking just like any of their outside sales colleagues. On their side, sales executives are equally accountable for the demo outcome as their sales consultants.

 **Recommendation:**

I have personally met and worked with many sales professionals, and I cannot say I have ever come to unconditionally love any, but I have for sure experienced friction with a few! All jokes aside, even today, whenever I interact with my sales executives, I try hard to walk in their shoes and understand the struggles they might have already faced trying to find out whatever piece of information they decided to delegate to me. I always push for more qualification, but I have become smart enough to understand when the sales rep has hit a wall, the only thing we can do is perform a demo even with the little information we were able to gather. Maybe we are late to the selection and the prospect cannot dedicate too much time to us, or maybe they have a crazy schedule that we have to accommodate. Or they are requiring us to re-build their same solution in our offering without being open to suggestions or changes. These are all circumstances that are hard for a salesperson to control or even change. We could argue that one should have started the sales cycle much sooner, or that one should have established such a good rapport with the prospect so they wouldn't deny us information and guidance. Reality, though, is not theory; it is not perfect. I have come to learn when to push back and when to agree on a less-than-desirable plan, and my judging parameter is very simple: how the sales reps typically collaborate with presales. Salespeople that are sensitive to my requests and come to me anticipating my questions will not receive a hard time if on a particular occasion they need me to jump on a sudden presentation without any additional indication (definitely against my usual request for deep qualification before any demo). Sales professionals that instead tend to act frantic or find shortcuts to push the workload off their shoulders will receive more push back, resulting in the opposite of their initial intention, which is deal stagnation.

Personality Traits of Salespeople

When dealing with sales reps, we should also try to remember three distinctive characteristics of any account executive's personality. Commonly, salespeople are:

- Emotionally Resilient. Salespeople have a tough job and yet they are goal-oriented and persistent in their endeavors. Top Account Executives know how to bounce back from a dry spell. They don't get discouraged when the sales numbers are down, but rather look for innovative ways to turn things around. Tenacity is in their DNA, and they do not give up until they meet their quota.

- Surprisingly Introvert. Salespeople are usually more concerned with people liking them than they are getting their customers to respect them. Most times than not, salespeople shy away from healthy confrontation because they are afraid of receiving "No" as an answer and are usually in desperate need of approval. I remember one of my sales coworkers once debriefing on how bad a reference call went because our current customer told the prospect evaluating our solution that they did not use our product for one of the five reasons the prospect wanted to chat about. To the sales rep's eyes, this sounded like a complete failure and the whole six-month sales cycle was now in jeopardy. Understandably, the greatest confidence boost to a salesperson's self-esteem is a sale, even better if above forecast. The opposite stands true as well, however: salespeople that spend many months without making a sale tend to panic, and panic induces desperation, leding the sales rep to chase phantom opportunities that are not a good fit and do not translate into any closed deal (negatively affecting the salesperson's win rate). Most importantly, desperation prevents the account executive from focusing on and pursuing legitimate opportunities.

- <u>Prima Donnas</u>. Salespeople are high maintenance, both when they close deals and when they do not. They are very well aware of their importance in any organization (there is no business without sales, in 95% of cases) and they are vocal about their requests and frustrations because they know they will be heard. This stands particularly true for the top performers of any sales organization: the more successful the salesperson, the more attention they require. Best way to handle it? Listen to their demands for your next demo, but do not give up ownership of your show; if you have to, keep them accountable and have them deal with the consequences!

True Story: Let It Fail

I remember once dealing with one of our best salespeople that wanted to go into a demo with a presentation flow that made absolutely no sense, claiming he had a better understanding of the prospect's situation. After explaining to my superstar why I disagreed three times, I agreed to his strategy, stating very clearly we would fail. One of my sales engineers did the demo following my top salesperson's suggestion and it ended up being a disaster. During our forecast review call, he admittedly said he jeopardized the deal by venturing into an area in which he had no expertise.

- <u>Not Necessarily Team Players.</u> Sales reps have a quota, or just like the saying goes, they are "coin-operated." I find this approach extremely rewarding for an organization with salespeople that are more "hunters" than "farmers." Usually, their variable compensation is linked to how much revenue the account executives bring to the table as individual contributors, unlike many other departments that have some, if not all, of their variable compensation linked to the overall company's performance. This compensation approach makes them almost lone wolves in the organization: they are always on the lookout for the next big deal because they know the return will be appealing. They usually see other members of the organization as an extension of their own arms and often tend to dictate how things should be done to maximize their individual profits. Not every sales rep should feel the right to be coin-operated in an organization because not *all* of them are hunters. Some sales reps have more of a "farmers" approach and do a good job with the support of a structure that feeds them work they can execute. In this case, they are more tied to the entire team, supporting them for obvious reasons.

- Passionately Competitive: good sales executives fear the leader board and want to be up on the podium measuring their skills against their peers. They don't just want to get better at what they do: They want to be better than everyone else.

Sales and Presales Coordination

The structure of the team and the interaction between sales representatives and sales engineers varies a lot based on the size of the organization and the product both teams have to represent.

Sales engineering is understandably seen as a function of Sales; therefore, both sales engineering and outside sales report to a Sales Director. While I understand the logic, I am not a huge fan of sales engineers reporting to the same sales director that manages the field sales executives. On top of this, I am totally against having sales engineers report to account executives. The two positions have the same goals but are in charge of different activities and take action in the sales cycle at different times. Not to mention that both positions sometimes experience friction with each other. Sales engineers judgmentally believe their sales reps constantly drop the ball and are not on top of their activities, while sales reps worry that their presales coworkers might derail the deal by showing off too much technical knowledge. Even from a purely organizational standpoint, sales and presales usually have a different compensation package but depend reciprocally on each other.

Given these typical traits, it is recommended to keep the two teams separate, maximizing their natural friction and demanding strong collaboration. A sales manager that has the right sensitivity to both worlds should be able to do this. Instead, a sales manager that has never been on the "engineering" side of the sales equation should either assume a mindset to develop such sensitivity or humbly request they report to a different team (General Management, Professional Services, Customer Success, etc.)

Especially in the era of Cloud SaaS technologies, I have seen Sales Engineering being more and more part of the Customer Success team. I personally tend to agree with this approach for two reasons:

- It augments the SEs' perception as trusted advisors whose main goal is advising the prospective customers on how to achieve success with the products and solutions they are demonstrating

- It naturally prompts for more constructive collaboration and increased transparency between the sales engineers and their sales counterparts, not having to worry too much about political reporting lines

No matter the hierarchical organization of the two teams, it is vital that there is strong alignment between sales engineering and outside sales. The two teams have to work constantly together and strategize on the winning approach to be as effective as possible on any deal they work on.

True Story: Specialization without Compromise

In my career as a Head of Presales reporting directly into the General Manager, I have run a team of several professionals, and I have always tried to find the right blend between specialization and flexibility. My team was a full national team across two oceans, so territory alignment between sales and presales was a given. Within each territory, however, I have stayed away from heavy team specializations, rotating my sales engineers across multiple sales reps as needed. At any request for a demo, I made it a habit for the sales rep to submit an electronic request to give me some basic information so I could assign the best resource to that sales cycle. Based on that information—which included the industry we were demoing to, the competition we would be up against, and some other details—I assigned the best fit for that opportunity, keeping in mind the industry expertise of my sales engineers and personality traits to maximize the outcome of the presentation. This allowed me to make sure that each opportunity was always staffed with the best resources, increasing our overall chances of doing well. It also allowed both the sales executives and the sales engineers to learn from each other and re-use that experience when they worked with somebody else within the team.

Aligning presales engineers with their sales counterparts should follow multiple criteria. Obviously, geography plays a huge role (containing expenses and maximizing communication); however, the two teams could also be aligned by industry or target company size.

Maybe some sales executives have specific knowledge in an industry that is also the domain of a sales engineer, and the two would be extremely effective together in a sales cycle. Or, the natural inclination and personality traits of some sales engineers make them more suitable to work on a specific target of organizations to balance off the opposite personality of a field salesperson.

Aligning salespeople and sales engineers has natural pros, such as allowing the two individuals to get to know each other to the point that one could predict what the other will say in a specific circumstance. Using the metaphor of a well-oiled machine, this approach also has a major con. Stagnation could be the downfall: exclusively working with the same team will not allow either the sales executive or the presales professional to learn from the experience that potentially pairing with a different teammate could give them.

A Few Requests for All Our Sales Friends!

Presales and Sales must work together and have each other's back with one ultimate goal: book the sale.

True Story: Sales & Presales Partnership

The Sales VP of our operation in the DACH region is a seasoned professional that in a few years has built one of the most performing markets for my company. During one of our annual kick-off meetings, he shared a story that caught my attention. The local Rep had just received a long list of requirements, with one request being to build multiple complicated use cases from scratch in our product and present them back to the customer's full evaluation team in just two days. The amount of work for the sales engineer would be immense. Our Sales VP jumped on the phone with the prospective customer saying they would not be able to deliver what was requested in just two days and asked for more time. The prospective customer responded that all of the other vendors had no complaints, therefore they would not give us any extra time. At that point, our Sales VP said that they would not bid for their business. Most importantly, he articulated no one should be expected to compete under such expectations. The explanation was so relevant for the prospective customer that they gave us seven more business days to work on the custom POC, and the DACH team ended up winning the deal. In our Win Report, we heard the customer saying it was all about the credibility that was perceived when we pushed back and explained what it would take to do things properly.

Since this is a handbook on the side of Presales professionals, here are a few asks that you, account executives, might or might have not heard about already.

Here is your SE talking right into your ear!

- <u>Deal Qualification:</u> I have spent a lot of time covering this topic, but it will never be enough. The more you salespeople spend your time gathering vital preliminary information on the competition—key players, political map, overall key pain points, and all of the other topics we have covered in the very first pages of this guide—the more efficient you can expect us, the Demo Gurus, to be. The only way to book a sale is to fix a challenge that a prospective customer is experiencing. Help us uncover what that challenge is and who is most affected by it and we will be incisive, sharp, and on point during our talk!

- <u>Control of the Sales Cycle:</u> The biggest mistake you as a salesperson could make is thinking your customers are always right—even your prospective customers. When shopping for technology and software solutions, it is very common to find corporations that are willing to be educated and guided throughout their selection and purchase process. This stands true for both the most experienced organizations and the first-timers to vendor-selection initiatives. Being able to counsel and direct your prospective customers, pushing back when it's right to do so, will help increase your credibility as a person that knows what needs to be done, rather than being perceived as wanting to push them to a contract at all costs. I have heard the words Mutually-Agreed-Action-Plan many times from my sales co-workers. A MAAP is a fantastic idea: it is a plan that shows all the steps in the sales/purchase cycle that our prospective customers will have to go through, where tasks, owners, and due dates have been mutually agreed upon by the vendor and the purchaser. As time goes by, the salesperson will be providing updates and keeping his or her prospective customers on track, showing them how delays in the tasks they have both agreed upon could jeopardize their project. As I said, I have seen these MAAPs many times in my career; too bad I have only seen these valuable documents when interviewing salespeople!

- CRM: If you do not want to be called up every day by your SE to learn how a deal you are working on together is progressing, keep your customer relationship management system up to date! Good sales engineers care a lot about the progress of the opportunities they have worked on, fully aware that the ultimate owner of the sales cycle is the Sales Executive. That passion and fervor to know more should be not misinterpreted as the sales engineer stepping on the salesperson's feet; it is just a genuine sense of excitement and commitment that great Demo Gurus have. Keep doing everything you normally do when interacting with prospective customers—via email or even a phone call—and use the latest available technology to track that communication directly on your CRM system. Making sure the CRM contains all the various touchpoints you salespeople have had with the prospect while your Demo Gurus were not present is of tremendous value for when sales engineers have to get involved. The more they are informed about past conversations, comments, or even jokes, the more your assigned presales resource will be able to jump in on the initiative with full awareness of the goals, landscape, actors, and personalities of this opportunity.

- NO is a powerful answer. Research proves that "No" is the most underused word in a salesperson's vocabulary. It is so painful to pronounce that most times it's not even a full "No" but rather a more timid "not really." The customer, including any prospective customer, is not always right, but they know you are willing to do anything you can possibly do to get a check from them. As much as we try to be accommodating to book the sale, sometimes your best option to seal the deal is to put your foot down and politely say "No," contextualizing the reasoning behind your answer. Clients and prospective customers will appreciate you rejecting the requests they have made, provided that you explain to them why and offer up alternatives. If they are still convinced their request is valid, encourage them to talk to someone else besides you to hear another perspective as to why it is not a good idea. Don't be afraid of saying "No" to win a deal.

Just So You Know...

We love it when you:

- Close a deal. This is the highest recognition of all the hard work we have put in together as a team. As passionate individuals that take pride in what they do, we love contributing to our company's growth, so keep those "Ring the bell" emails coming!

- Can accommodate our schedule. It is a huge sign of respect and understanding of our job when salespeople will not agree on a presentation date without first talking to their presales consultant. Sometimes even that extra day to prepare an intense custom demo or full blown-out POC makes the difference in winning the deal.

- Show us a path to closing. As a clear sign of deal control, it is extremely beneficial for sales engineers to know what happens after our next demo. This will dictate the level of details the SE will go into, the style that needs to be used, and the type of information that needs to be conveyed.

We get cranky when you:

- Stay quiet during the demo. Help us out! Jump in, interject any time you feel we are not clear enough, study the room, and engage as much as you can. Feel free to participate in the meeting beyond the traditional 15-minute company overview and the 10-minute Q&A at the end. Make yourself an active attendee and presenter during our demo time; this will help make the overall presentation more dynamic, feel less like a lecture, and it will naturally drive engagement from other users as well.

- Come unprepared. We know you are busy. We all are. Please check the spelling on your PowerPoint presentation and eliminate all of the boiler-plate/corporate marketing slides that are not fully applicable to the opportunity we are working on and make them relevant for our prospective customer. Best example: get rid of that Manufacturing Case Study your Corporate Marketing Team is so proud of when you present to a Bank!

- Book our hotel. There is no need to book our hotels! As much as we appreciate you taking the time out of your busy schedule to book our rooms or flights, we like those points, too! Just tell us where you are staying and where we are meeting for dinner the night before, and we'll be there!

- Commit to a demo without asking. Our calendars might not always be up to date and we might have some non-client facing work that requires preparation (RFP, Proof of Concept, etc.) Please give us a ring before you book the next demo; chances are we will be able to confirm your preference, but we just want to avoid double booking.

Chapter 3.3 – Great Demo! But We Lost the Deal

Probably one of the most demotivating aspects of our job as Demo Gurus is when we know we have done a phenomenal job during our demo, but the prospective customer still decides to go with another vendor.

What makes it even more irritating is when, during the post-award debrief, customers openly state that we gave a "great demo" or that our presales resource did such a phenomenal job that the evaluation team would love to have him or her on their team. This type of feedback is frustrating to very pragmatic people like myself. If we did not win their business and somebody else did, well, that somebody else executed better than we did somewhere during the sales cycle.

It has happened to my team and me several times that we "rocked the demo," put it on the "ours to lose" whiteboard after a very commending email from the prospect, and then, for some unforeseen rationale, we did not win the deal. Usually, when that happens, it is due to one or more of the following reasons:

- <u>Lack of differentiation or value selling:</u> This usually happens when our demos, or more in general the overall sales cycle, is feature/function-oriented. In this case, we as Demo Gurus undeniably deliver exceptional technical presentations: we know our product, we know our technology, and we know our clicks. The same applies to our competitor's presales guru. We might be under the impression that we did great as we went through every single piece of functionality they had to score us on or that they mentioned in their discovery call. However, we were not able to differentiate ourselves from the competition (and it is fair to assume they had the same set of features). Most importantly, we were not able to translate how those features could make our prospects' lives easier. My best demos consist of me showing about five to eight screens of my software solution over 90 minutes. The rest of the time is spent connecting the dots between my product functionality and the customers' needs. All heavy, product-centric sales cycles should make us think about our ability to win, and even if we do, our ability to price our solution for the right value it could bring to our customers. As Presales professionals, we will do just fine in every "beauty-contest" type of selection; let's just not get our hopes high. Unless we elevate the process from pure product to value selling, chances are we will be disappointed when we hear our prospect's final decision.

- Price: How many times have you heard the inevitable comment, "You have a very good product, but it is just too expensive for us"? This situation is a predictable source of demotivation for any sales engineer as it intrinsically implies the opportunity has not been well qualified. When there is no qualification or even poor qualification, our chances of winning a deal are relegated to pure luck. We should never be hearing "price" as a reason for losing a deal: it is our salesperson's job and responsibility to make sure that the future customers we are working with have a budget allocated to their projects, and that it is adequate for our product. Even in specific cases when our solution is too expensive, I am sure Top Management would entertain a special discount. Maybe that prospective customer is instrumental for our organization to penetrate an industry in which we want to be exposed. Maybe it is just a logo we would love to add to our website, or maybe there is a huge, predictable upcoming revenue stream beyond the current initiative. Whatever the reason, presales should not be involved in any opportunity that the company is not ready to pursue because of pricing. Losing a deal for lack of diligent qualification is disrespectful and a huge waste of precious time (for both sides).

- **Focusing on the wrong audience:** This has happened to me a few times. This scenario refers to all those cases where we believe specific people in the room will be in charge of the final decision, but at the end of the selection process, we find out they were the spokesman for a different group of people. This goes back to carefully understanding the political map within an organization and understanding their buying process. What is important to remember, however, is that during a demonstration, sales engineers should try to focus on all attendees in the room, giving them proper attention and winning as many people over as they can. Focusing on the decision makers is vital; however, ignoring the rest of the team will have a negative effect even if the sponsor were to prefer our solution. Unless you are dealing with very dominant personalities that are ready to go against the common guidance of their team and risk the outcome of their choice, it is unusual to find a decision maker that won't listen to his or her teams' opinion. As already discussed, the more collaborative decision-making processes in today's work environments makes it even harder for sales engineers as they have to "win everybody over." While this is a challenging task, it is what we should always aim for. If most of the audience believes in our solution, the decision makers will be reassured in their selection.

- **Misreading your audience:** Far too often I have heard this comment when I ask my sales engineers how a specific demonstration went: *"I think it went well. They were very quiet, but we showed them everything they asked for, and they seemed to be okay with that."* This is a TOTAL misinterpretation of the situation. Your demonstration did not go well—it was probably average. Yes, you passed their checklist and you tackled all of their points, but you were not able to engage your audience. Your audience was "quiet the whole time," meaning they were not particularly interested or were not seeing the value in how your solution could address their main points. The reaction you can expect from your audience can vary a lot depending on multiple factors, industry education of your prospective customers being one of those. First timers to software selections tend to be wowed with very basic features and functions that are probably a standard in your competitive landscape just because they do not have enough knowledge of market offerings. However, they soon will realize it is more of a common requirement in the industry as they continue with their selection process. You should keep this in mind and not get overly optimistic about this type of situation. Cultural background and geography could also play an important role in properly "reading a room." With all the exceptions that any generalization always implies, people in New York City are usually more vocal than their quieter co-workers in Iowa; I would not necessarily leave the room with a negative impression if the attendees in Iowa were not interrupting me every two sentences with additional requests.

- **No real deal:** It happens. Sometimes we are called to compete in a specific software selection, and we understand only at the end that there was no real selection to start with! The prospect had already made up their mind on the vendor from whom they wanted to buy but had to open up a selection just for pure due diligence or simply to make their procurement department happy. No matter how great your demo is, there are very few chances that you and your sales counterpart will ever close that deal. These are not easy scenarios to detect, since no prospective customer will ever tell you exactly what the reality is. There are, however, some hints that should get you and your team thinking. Typically, this happens when one of the newly appointed decision makers already has had a good experience with one of your top competitors in their past work experiences. He/she knows it would be a safe choice to do well in the new role while reducing risk. Similarly, understanding the political map could unveil some relationship between the top management of your prospective customer and the higher ranks of one of your competitors. Probably the most revealing sign of lack of real interest is exactly that; when the potential customers do not make themselves available for discovery calls or are hard to get on the phone to discuss more about their project with you. Someone genuinely interested in their selection initiative will find time to give all vendors the same battleground so the company can assess which vendor shines the best, all things being equal. When there is no real commitment from the customer's side in having your organization succeed, you should seriously consider the genuineness of their selection process.

- **Politics:** out of all the scenarios illustrated so far, when it comes down to politics, there is very little that the sales team can do to change the decision unless you are on the lucky side of the equation! In this case, no matter how phenomenal your demo performance was, it is very hard that your team will win the deal. Politics usually happen at the highest levels, typically involving executives from both the customer and the provider side. All it takes is a personal relationship between your prospect's CFO and your competitor's CEO to derail your sales efforts and minimize your chances of winning the deal. It is not easy to prevent these situations when they happen. The most you can do is to prepare for it by flawlessly understanding the buying process and dominating the political map by researching your decision-makers' past experiences and connections to your competitor's C-level.

True Story: The Deceitful Board Member!

I have always received commending feedback on my product demonstrations. In one of my last demonstrations as a proud Demo Guru, I had the CFO of a California based company come and shake my hand at the end of the meeting. I even received private notes from attendees of the demonstration to congratulate me on my way back to the airport. The audience jokingly asked a few times if I were to be part of the implementation team and even found multiple "you rock" text messages from my own sales team on my phone when I turned it back on after the demo. Still, we lost the deal. After a painful debrief with our business sponsor, we found out that when our name was brought up to the Executive Board as the selected software vendor for their upcoming initiative, one of the board members chimed in and asked to re-evaluate a competitive solution. The board member insisted she had successfully done work specifically with a gentleman from the competition that she utterly trusted and organized herself another meeting with the entire team and the initially-disqualified vendor. Obviously, we tried a few times to get on the board member's calendar, without success. We sent notes and explanations to the entire selection committee, including the company CEO, to explain the unfair treatment we were receiving. That was not enough to have a professional chat with the board member who, only 6 months after the selection process was over, also joined our competitor's board of directors!

Conclusions

Being a Demo Guru is fun. I recommend experiencing this profession to anyone that enjoys evangelizing how software technology can create compelling solutions to address both the most complex and the most trivial challenges organizations routinely face.

Being a Demo Guru is stressful. You are constantly on stage, always in the spotlight, and usually are the one and only one talking while many are listening. You need to show confidence while feeling butterflies in your stomach, you need to listen while controlling your adrenaline, and you need to think about your next move while listening.

Being a Demo Guru is rewarding. You will experience many gratifying moments as a Sales Engineer: from the moment when the prospective customer agrees to sign the deal only if YOU are part of their product implementation to the moment when the top executive in the room asks you a question and then shakes your hand, congratulating you at the end of the presentation.

To all the Demo Gurus out there, as I always say at the end of my presentations, "I hope you found this content informative, but let me leave you with a few main points I think are critical to reiterate from today's conversations":

- Listen to your customers' needs and focus on what they want, not what you want. If you went to a steakhouse and asked for that steak you've been craving, and then the waiter brings you a salmon, how would you react?

- Research, prepare, and practice. Enough is not enough. Do your homework, study your prospect, invest time in learning more about them, and prepare as much as you can to prove to them that your solution is the best fit in the market to help them not only today but also in the future.

- Collaborate with your sales reps. You are a team and both of you want to be successful in closing as many deals as possible. Talk to your sales counterparts, strategize together, and learn how to interact together during the sales cycle.

- Do not lie. Sales is not about lying. Stretch your software capabilities only if you are confident your product can get there in some way, but never say YES when the answer should be a positive, confident NO.

- Less is more. Sales engineering is not training. Avoid going into any painful amount of details that your audience is not requiring at that very second and provide more information only on demand.

Have fun!

Further Reading & Watching

As part of my career in Presales and as a source of inspiration for this book, I have enjoyed the experience and education of many colleagues globally that have shared their experiences in the form of written handbooks, blogs, communities, forums, and podcasts.

Below are some recommended materials for further education and enjoyment.

Books:

- *Mastering Technical Sales: The Sales Engineer's Handbook*. John Care, Aron Bohlig. Artech House.

- *Bury my heart at Conference Room B*. Stan Slap. Portfolio.

- *Great Demo! How To Create And Execute Stunning Software Demonstrations*. Peter E. Cohen. iUniverse.

- *The Science of Selling: Proven Strategies to Make Your Pitch, Influence Decisions, and Close the Deal*. David Hoffeld. TarcherPerigee.

- *The Little Prince*. Antoine de Saint-Exupéry. Mariner Books.

- *Virtual Selling: How to Build Relationships, Differentiate, and Win Sales Remotely*. Mike Schultz, Dave Shaby, Andy Springer. 35 Group Press.

Online Communities/Podcasts/Blogs/Forums:

- *Presales Collective*. https://www.presalescollective.com

- *The Modern SC*. https://themodernsc.com

- *Sales Hacker*. https://www.saleshacker.com

- *National Society of Sales Engineers*. https://www.nationalsse.com

- *We the Sales Engineers*. https://wethesalesengineers.com

Glossary of Acronyms and Abbreviations

ABM	Activity Based Marketing
AE	Account Executive
ARR	Annual Recurring Revenue
B2B	Business to Business
BANT	Budget, Authority, Need, Timeline
BI	Business Intelligence
CEO	Chief Executive Officer
CFO	Chief Financial Officer
CPM	Corporate Performance Management
CRM	Customer Relationship Manager
CS	Customer Success
EPM	Enterprise Performance Management
ERP	Enterprise Resource Planning
GM	General Manager
HQ	Headquarter
IT	Information Technology
MAAP	Mutually Agreed Action Plan
MQL	Marketing Qualified Lead
POC	Proof of Concept
PS	Professional Services
Q&A	Questions & Answers
QA	Quality Assurance
QBR	Quarterly Business Review
QSO	Qualified Sales Opportunity
RFI	Request for Information
RFP	Request for Proposal
SAAS	Software as a Service
SC	Sales Consultant
SDR	Sales Development Representative
SE	Sales Engineer
SEO	Search Engine Optimization
SME	Subject Matter Expert(ise)

SML	Spontaneous Memory Loss
SQL	Sales Qualified Lead
TCO	Total Cost of Ownership
VOC	Vendor of Choice

About the Author

Alessio Lolli is a veteran in cloud technologies with a diverse cultural background and a passion for empowering organizations through the adoption of modern software solutions.

In his 15+ years of hands-on experience as a Demo Guru, Alessio has met with thousands of global C-level executives as well as line managers who inspire him to always look at any matter from at least two perspectives.

Alessio is currently leading the efforts for a NA cloud software company. Given his "foodie" temper, he could not be living anywhere else but New York City.

Index of Tables & Figures

Tables

Figures

NOTES

NOTES

NOTES

NOTES

NOTES

NOTES

NOTES

NOTES

NOTES

NOTES

NOTES

Printed in the United States
By Bookmasters